SUBVERSIVE ORTHODOXY

SUBVERSIVE ORTHODOXY

OUTLAWS, REVOLUTIONARIES,
AND OTHER CHRISTIANS IN DISGUISE

ROBERT INCHAUSTI

BrazosPress

Grand Rapids, Michigan

© 2005 by Robert Inchausti

Published by Brazos Press
a division of Baker Publishing Group
P.O. Box 6287, Grand Rapids, MI 49516-6287
www.brazospress.com

Printed in the United States of America

Library of Congress Cataloging-in-Publication Data
Inchausti, Robert, 1952-
    Subversive orthodoxy : outlaws, revolutionaries, and other Christians in disguise / Robert Inchausti.
        p.   cm.
    Includes bibliographical references and index.
    ISBN 1-58743-087-8 (pbk.)
    1. Christianity and culture. 2. Christianity—Influence. I. Title.
BR115.C8I475 2005
270.8—dc22   2004020689

For Linda, Monica, and Nick

John said to him, "Teacher, we saw someone casting out de-mons in your name, and we tried to stop him, because he was not following us." But Jesus said, "Do not stop him; for no one who does a deed of power in my name will be able soon after-ward to speak evil of me. Whoever is not against us is for us."

Mark 9:38–40

Contents

Introduction

We are living in the greatest revolution in history—a huge
spontaneous upheaval of the entire human race: not the revo-
lution planned and carried out by any particular party, race,
or nation, but a deep elemental boiling over of all the inner
contradictions that have ever been in man, a revelation of
the chaotic forces inside everybody. This is not something
we have chosen, nor is it something we are free to avoid.

    This revolution is a profound spiritual crisis of the whole world,
manifested largely in desperation, cynicism, violence, conflict,
self-contradiction, ambivalence, fear and hope, doubt and belief,
creation and destructiveness, progress and regression, obsessive
attachments to images, idols, slogans, programs that only dull the
general anguish for a moment until it bursts out everywhere in
a still more acute and terrifying form. We do not know if we are
building a fabulously wonderful world or destroying all that we
have ever had, all that we have achieved! All the inner force of
man is boiling and bursting out, the good together with the evil,
the good poisoned by evil and fighting it, the evil pretending to
be good and revealing itself in the most dreadful crimes, justified
and rationalized by the purest and most innocent intentions.

Thomas Merton, *Conjectures of a Guilty By-Stander*[1]

1. Thomas Merton, *Conjectures of a Guilty By-Stander* (Garden City, N.Y.: Doubleday, 1966), 54–55.

Over the past seventy-five years, the Gospels have served as a pivot around which many of the most trenchant analyses of modern civilization have turned. And yet there remains a persistent misconception that Christianity is inherently reactionary, unconsciously wedded to class, race, and gender prejudices, bound by foundational metaphysics, and littered with outworn superstitions.

It is easy to understand why so many people think this way. The media showers attention on the most extreme and sensational expressions of the faith, while the work of serious Christian thinkers spans such a variety of disciplines that it's very hard to track. This book attempts to correct this error by taking a hard and sustained look at those macrohistorians, social activists, and avant-garde novelists whose unique contributions to secular thought derive from their Christian worldviews.

None of these figures is strictly speaking a theologian, and yet if there is any significant theological breakthrough on the horizon, it must be found here—in the refreshed, battle-hardened spirituality of Christian thinkers operating within secular contexts whose individual accomplishments testify against the worldwide acquiescence to economic "realities," military "imperatives," and so-called geopolitical necessities.

In other words, the work of each of these thinkers proves that the quaint collection of unfashionable religious absolutes—what used to be called "Christian humanism"—has not stood idly by amidst all the attacks leveled upon it by fundamentalists and cultural materialists. On the contrary, it has survived and thrived—quietly absorbing the blows, navigating the philosophical backwaters, weathering the political storms, and offering up its own (if largely misunderstood) critique of the contemporary world.

This new breed of theoretically savvy Christian humanists are not apologists for the status quo, but subversive—inherently suspicious of worldly power and actively working for a more just world. For them, the postmodern culture critics Michel Foucault and Jacques Derrida got it only half right. Yes, the Enlightenment project was narrowly conceived, but that doesn't mean that the best alternative to it is an even more theoretically self-conscious hyperrationalism. For even if Western civilization is built upon metaphysical assumptions that privilege men over women, "presence" over "absence," and "speech" over "writing," that doesn't mean that the best way to compensate for these distortions is by politicizing our thinking even more.

On the contrary, the figures examined here argue for exactly the reverse procedure: the "depoliticizing" of thought altogether through the creation of shared contemplative "space" made available by a return to an eschatological perspective on human existence—a perspective that examines all thought and culture in terms of how they would appear in the messianic light of the Last Day.

In other words, they subject everything to the cleansing fire of an eschatological perspective on existence. This strategy puts them in a peculiar and, from my point of view, privileged position from which to assess the transition we are all currently experiencing from the modern to the millennial mind. Unlike cognitive scientists, such as Marvin Minsky and Stephen Pinker, they do not believe that "calculation" has become our master metaphor and method.[2] For them, myth—as the mode of simultaneous awareness of multiple causes and effects—remains at the heart of human self-understanding and, properly understood, is capable of renewing our culture and transforming the Enlightenment disciplines from the inside out.

Elie Wiesel, author, Noble Peace Prize winner, and Holocaust survivor, once described our current spiritual situation this way:

> A few hundred years ago, Man asked God if he could switch places with Him for just a few seconds, so that he could know what it was like to be God, and God could know what it was like to be a man.

2. For an introduction to these ideas, see *The New Humanists,* ed. John Brockman (New York: Barnes & Noble, 2003).

God declined the offer, explaining that once man became God, he might not want to change back.

But Man insisted that he only wanted to taste omnipotence for a just few moments.

So God agreed, and the change was made.

But Man refused to give up his power.

And since that time, Man has been God, and God has been Man.

Just recently have both parties become unbearably uncomfortable with the whole arrangement.[3]

The thinkers examined in this book have all grown unbearably uncomfortable with the current metaphysical arrangements. Each reimagines the Judeo-Christian epic in global, transcultural, and macrohistorical terms and in the process refigures our relationship to God and our place in the cosmos.

What follows is an extended essay that links their views into a single, as yet largely unacknowledged, tradition that I call, for lack of a better term, "the orthodox avant-garde." This "tradition" consists of cutting-edge Christian thinkers who, merely by expressing the contemporary moral and intellectual implications of their faith, have exposed the dogmas of modernism in the light of a more inclusive and liberating Christian vision of reality.

By telling their stories and explaining their perspectives, I hope to awaken Christians to the contemporary wing of their own prophetic tradition—especially those who, from simple inattention, have never noticed the contributions Christian thinkers have made to the cutting edge of contemporary thought. But I also hope to challenge those suspicious of religious assumptions altogether into reconsidering the powerful insights that can emerge when one takes seriously the paradox of the incarnation and the scandal of the cross.

This book, therefore, is not about *new* religious values so much as it is about the eternal freshness of the old ones. Most of the thinkers examined

3. Quoted in Harold Kushner, *Who Needs God?* (New York: Fireside Books, 2002), 58.

here are religious traditionalists whose ideas challenge the assumptions of their secular colleagues. Most are also innovators in their respective fields, alert to contemporary circumstances, aware of changes in their disciplines, critical of the dominant narratives, and yet still capable of drawing connections between their faith and the realities of the modern world.

Each of them does far more than simply say "no" to modernism; they bridge the chasm between our longings for spiritual completion and the technoscientific world within which we live. From Andy Warhol[4] to Marshall McLuhan, this orthodox avant-garde finds its inspiration not only in the Gospels, but in the monastic silences of John Cage,[5] the devotional music of John Coltrane,[6] even the negative dialectics of Theodore Adorno.[7] Of course, they don't adopt the views of these figures without critique but transform them in the light of their faith. And, this, finally, is the subject and substance of this book: the impact this unrecognized cadre of avant-garde Christian humanists have had—or *should* have had—upon both Christian theology and contemporary thought.

But I am getting ahead of my story here, so let's back up a bit to take a look at those who prepared the way for this unexpected return to religious vision—the Christian "Romantics" and their turn-of-the-century descendents, the Russian dissidents.

4. Jane Daggett Dillenberg's *The Religious Art of Andy Warhol* (New York: Continuum, 1998) makes a surprisingly strong case for Warhol's crypto-Catholicism—pointing out, among other things, that he attended mass several times a week, worked in a soup kitchen (disguised in a brown wig he purchased especially for these occasions), prayed daily with his mother, who was a Byzantine Catholic, kept a crucifix and devotional book by his bed, and produced more than one hundred drawings and paintings of the Last Supper. His famous serial paintings of Marilyn Monroe grew out of his interest in religious iconography and his preoccupation with the dead and the afterlife.

5. Although only in part a reflection on John Cage, see Jack Miles's telling reflection "Global Requiem" in the fall 2000 issue of *Cross Currents*.

6. For a look at Coltrane's Christian spirituality, see the essay on Coltrane in Rodney Clapp's *Border Crossings* (Grand Rapids: Brazos Press, 2000) and Ashley Kahn's book *A Love Supreme: The Story of John Coltrane's Signature Album* (New York: Viking, 2002).

7. S. Buck-Morss in *The Origin of Negative Dialectics* (New York: Free Press, 1977) tells us that Theodore Adorno came very close to converting to Catholicism in his early twenties. No one, as far as I know, has explored the connection this might have to his criticism of Kierkegaard in his first book or to the mystical leanings in his later thought.

1

The Soul under Siege

*The toughest struggle of all is to try and meld the sacred and the
profane, the natural and the supernatural, this world and the next.
Admit to this preoccupation and you're in deep trouble with your
church and your state. Try to make a record of it, as did St. Augustine, or St. John of the Cross, or William Blake, and you're scorned
and, perhaps, imprisoned by your contemporaries, even if later
generations regard you—usually without reading you—as a classic.*

Jim Christy, *The Long, Slow Death of Jack Kerouac*[1]

he thinkers that prefigure the orthodox avant-garde were mostly
conservative outsiders working from Christian premises *against* the
appropriations of the sacred by the Enlightenment Rationalists and *for*
the renewal of the faith through the power of revelation. If one were to
trace these countercultural thinkers back to their sources, one would
find that they all begin in "back-to-basics" movements of one sort or

---

1. Jim Christy, *The Long, Slow Death of Jack Kerouac* (Toronto: ECW Press, 1998), 91–92.

another. Zen, according to the Buddhist scholar Roger Corliss, was a "back to Bodi" movement, just as Monasticism, the Reformation, and the Counter-Reformation were all "back-to-Jesus" movements of one kind or another. In each of these cases, revelation exposed the fossilized conventions at the heart of a dying cultural system. In each instance transcendent reality became more palpable than worldly certainties, driving the religious traditions back to their sources and giving birth to radically new ideas and practices.

The history of living religion, as opposed to the history of its cultural forms, is the history of the soul's challenges to various established rites and orders that have tried to usurp the untethered existential authority of revelation. By *revelation*, I simply mean the experience of something that transcends the givens of everyday experience, an insight or experience that simply cannot be reduced to or explained by anything that has gone before. In other words, the history of faith is really the story of how the soul outdistances its own culture-bound rituals —refurbishing itself from the inside out through the examples of its prophets and saints. Zen koans, for example, are not epistemological riddles, as our Enlightenment philosophers might describe them, but exemplary forms of poetic revivification like the Sermon on the Mount. They preserved the spiritual content of a tradition by challenging convention on the invisible wings of metaphor.

In his book *The Everlasting Man*, G. K. Chesterton describes the power of orthodoxy to renew itself, in a chapter titled "Five Deaths of the Faith."[2] Christianity, he tells us, was never really reborn, because it never really died. The cultures it lived in died, so Christianity was rediscovered five times in the history of the West, as one cultural epoch was superseded by another. This happened after the fall of Rome, then in the twelfth century at the end of the feudal era, again when the medieval synthesis gave way to the secular energies of the Renaissance, again when the Renaissance fell to the new rationalism of the Enlightenment, and yet

2. G. K. Chesterton, *The Everlasting Man* (Ft. Collins, Colo.: Ignatius Press, 1993), 250.

again as Enlightenment values have begun to dissolve with the arrival of our postindustrial age.

In each instance, the end of civilization and death of God were proclaimed—but what was really dying was a complex set of institutional arrangements wedded to particular cultural premises. In each case, a new cultural age emerged when Christianity was rediscovered as something above and beyond the culture that claimed to embody it. It wasn't that the faith *evolved* to fit the times, nor did it exactly *conquer*. It was more that after each subsequent culture faced up to its illusions and its misrepresentations of the creed, orthodoxy simply reemerged whole cloth out of the ashes of history: unscathed, clarified, and renewed.

We are undergoing just such a reemergence of Christianity on the far side of cultural modernism. Our five-hundred-year fascination with calculation is withering on the lonely, dissipated vine of the disseminated postmodern "self." The contemporary interest in Gnosticism—the idea that our true divinity is blocked from our awareness by a particular cultural ignorance—answers the need contemporary believers have for a rigorous critique of existing religious institutions. Made attractive by eloquent apologists such as Elaine Pagels and Harold Bloom, this view reminds us that traditional church doctrines are themselves built upon the shifting sands of long-lost theological debates and ecclesiastical compromises, and that, in the end, the collection of doctrines, dogmas, and beliefs that we currently call orthodox were one of the many roads open to the faith during those fluid first few centuries of Christianity.[3]

The Gnostics argue that the orthodox path is not necessarily the right one, whereas most of the figures examined here remind us that it's not necessarily the wrong one either. And I suspect what we are really witnessing in the current fascination with lost spiritual traditions is more a symptom of an abiding interest in the lost wisdom of Christian orthodoxy than any outright rejection of it. The fascination with unconventional sources and lost gospels, not unlike the fundamentalists' fascination with

---

3. See, for example, Elaine Pagels's fascinating book *The Gnostic Gospels* (New York: Vintage, 1989) and Harold Bloom's *Breaking the Vessels* (Chicago: University of Chicago Press, 1982).

biblical inerrancy, is part of the same desire to ground Christian revelation upon some tangible positivist absolute, to break the life cycle of cultural birth and death to arrive at some unshakable, human absolute.

But this is not going to happen. The incarnation, like the resurrection, and like the very notion of divinity itself, cannot be reduced to a precept, fact, or theory; nor is it even, strictly speaking, a doctrine. It is, rather, a revelation that must be experienced in order to be understood, a reality wrapped in a mystery inside an enigma, miniaturized into a narrative that proves itself apodictically true by the realities it reveals. The false knowledge that blocks our capacity to experience this shift in awareness from the mundane to the sublime changes from epoch to epoch and from place to place, and this is why myth, rather than logic, is the only means through which the sublime can be expressed.

Faith, for the modern skeptic, is seen as an inability to doubt, and therefore a form of ignorance, if not outright stupidity. But for the Christian, faith is the capacity to grasp the significance of the Christian mythos as something more than merely a moral/intellectual construct. It is the capacity to see in the life of Christ both a literal and a figurative delineation of humanity's relationship to God. When "believers" talk to skeptics, they use images, tell stories, and give signs in an attempt to break through their culturally bound vision and lack of imaginative reach. But when the skeptics talk back, they flatfootedly translate those narratives into concepts, thereby misreading story as argument and hence focusing upon the seeming logical contradictions.

This is, perhaps, why skeptics attribute all kinds of odd ideas and beliefs to religious souls that have absolutely nothing to do with what they actually think. It's as if the skeptics cannot grasp myth as anything other than false belief, and so they miss entirely the metaconceptual aspects of faith—taking its figures literally and falsely projecting metaphysical notions upon what is essentially a poetic and deeply ironic worldview.

The Gnostics describe this miscommunication in terms of a systematically distorted or lost transcendental tradition, whereas the orthodox see it more in terms of a perpetually shifting set of historical circumstances.

In either case, communicating the Christian mythos as something macrohistorical will always be inherently problematic, for we are always left on our own to a consideration of the meaning the Christian revelation holds for *our* times, *our* realities, *our* frames of reference, *our* science, *our* morality, and *our*selves: problems of application and personal interpretation from which even the most deft historical reconstructions or biblical exegeses cannot save us.

In our era, just as in every transitional age, God *seems* dead, but it is really our Enlightenment culture that has died. Our old shared realities are giving way to new forms and new institutions. God, however, is radically independent of such "worldly" scenarios. We are the ones who are changing.

This is what William Blake tried to tell us, and what Goethe and Kierkegaard so deeply understood.

William Blake's Defense of the Imagination

> Critics say his [Blake's] visions were false because he was mad. I say he was mad because his visions were true.
>
> G. K. Chesterton, *William Blake*[4]

> Blake restored to me my earlier raptures, to my true vocation, that of lover.
>
> Czeslaw Milosz, *The Land of Ulro*[5]

If one were to seek the great archetypal precursor for prophetic Christian thinkers championing the soul's return from the spiritual exile of Enlightenment rationalism, then William Blake comes very close to casting the mold. Condemned as heretical by some and as too orthodox by

---

4. G. K. Chesterton, *William Blake* (London: Duckworth, 1910), 94.
5. Czeslaw Milosz, *The Land of Ulro*, trans. Louis Iribarne (New York: Farrar, Straus, & Giroux, 1984), 31.

others, he was one of the first to point out exactly how the new sciences were distorting the role of the imagination in human affairs and putting the soul to sleep. He tried to warn the emerging Cartesian mind that without contraries there is no progression and set out to demonstrate the paradoxical nature of truth through a series of poetic and artistic masterpieces that remain shocking and countercultural to this day.

Blake saw England much as Milton did, as a lapsed Christian nation in need of salvation and reform. Declaring himself a modern-day incarnation of the prophet Isaiah, he wrote:

> "I will not cease from Mental Fight
> Nor shall my sword sleep in my hand;
> Till we have built Jerusalem
> In England's green and pleasant land."[6]

The "mental fight" he engaged in was not a rhetorical battle with the powers and principalities of his day, but a bold counterassault against the emerging new epistemologies.

In *Radical Theology and the Death of God*, Thomas Altizer and William Hamilton described William Blake's contribution to Western thought:

> Blake was the first of the great modern seers. Through Blake *we can sense the theological significance of a poetic reversal of our mythical traditions,* and become open to the possibility that the uniquely modern metamorphosis of the sacred into the profane is the culmination of a redemptive and kenotic movement of the Godhead."[7]

This, I think, is an essentially accurate description of Blake's intellectual significance. I would, however, reverse the figure and the field. Blake does not celebrate the sacred *becoming profane* but *the profane becoming sacred.*

---

6. William Blake, *Selected Poetry and Prose,* ed. Northrop Frye (New York: Modern Library, 1953), 245.

7. Thomas J. J. Altizer and William Hamilton, *Radical Theology and the Death of God* (Indianapolis: Bobbs-Merrill, 1966), 16. Italics mine.

Christ turns the world on its head by overcoming the false distinctions inherent to any and all cultural mythologies—replacing the world's power structures and hierarchical "mental" constructs with the primacy of the soul. It struck Blake as one of the greatest ironies of Western history that at precisely the moment when political revolutions were putting the Christian ideal "into the street," European thinkers were throwing that same ideal out of their disciplines for a materialist metaphysic in which all life was reduced to the interplay of objects.

England, Blake argued, was losing its connection to the transcendent realm, replacing a scandalous, revolutionary faith in Christ with the respectable idol of pure reason. So England needed someone to stop this headlong rush into spiritual blindness. For Blake, the power-seeking, utilitarian mind was the very incarnation of self-absorption, out of touch with the spiritual energies of God and the revolutionary fervor of the age, and therefore evil. Blake, in other words, was "orthodox" in his prophetic stand against the new materialism, but "avant-garde" in his resistance to the abstract, distant, postponed, Watchmaker God of the Enlightenment theologians and scientists.

Contrary to the simplifications presented in schoolbooks and encyclopedias, Blake cannot be reduced to a "romantic," "antinomian," "Gnostic," "Mugglewump," "death-of-God theologian," or any of the other labels he's been saddled with over the years. To read him through any one of these lenses blinds you to the true originality—and utter simplicity—of his worldview. Blake wrote, "The Nature of my Work is Visionary or Imaginative; it is an Endeavor to restore what the Ancients called the Golden Age."[8] And although he failed to restore that age, his paintings and illuminated books give witness to its eternal significance.

Part of the reason Blake is sometimes misread as a Gnostic derives from the fact that he often used biblical imagery to express *literary* and political ideas—that is to say, he used Christian myths and images, speculative probes, poetic revivifications, and ironies to express his take on

---

8. William Blake, "A Vision of the Last Judgement," in Blake, *Selected Poetry and Prose,* 387.

the current events. His *Proverbs from Hell* is a case in point providing
the counterpoint and completion to the *Proverbs from Heaven* already
contained in the Bible. The appropriation of hell as part of God's creation
may sound like heresy to some, but it is more truly a reflection of Blake's
willingness to think through the distortions (indeed inversions) of the
Christian faith in his time. And if he sometimes presented humanity as
bound in a hostile world where the Spirit within was waiting for release,
he saw this more as *the particular crisis of the modern age*—not as a
metaphysical absolute. So when Blake remarks that "Reality is forgot &
the Vanities of Time & Space only remembered & called Reality," he is
speaking specifically of the spiritual state of Enlightenment England, not
the primordial state of man.

Blake was a spiritual exile whose life reflected the spiritual exile of his
nation and, through that, the spiritual exile of modern humanity. For Blake,
Christ had redeemed this world, but we had not yet learned how to bear
the beams of his love or act justly in the light of his sacrifice. And modern
trends in natural philosophy were taking us even further from that goal.

The aim of human life, he insisted, was not to become docile believers,
but to become capable of acts of spiritual genius made possible through
the attainment of a second innocence. This second innocence could
emerge only on the far side of worldly experience and corruption. And
in the modern era, that corruption cut to the core of our imaginative
selves. (He had no idea how much deeper the television, advertising, and
marketing industries would carry worldliness into the soul.)

Blake explained the fall of the imagination from direct revelation to
its recovery via the Gospels this way: "Let it here be noted that the Greek
Fables originated in Spiritual Mystery & Real Visions, which are lost and
clouded in Fable & Allegory, while the Hebrew Bible & the Greek Gospel
are Genuine, Preserved by the Savior's Mercy."[9] For him, the Hebrew Bible
and the Greek Gospels expressed the "true" eschatological meaning of
existence in the liberation of the human imagination from the blinders of

9. Ibid.

doubt and materialism. The so-called New Era was actually a return to a pagan fascination with "presence." In this sense, the full meaning of Blake's writings could really be appreciated only after Karl Marx exposed the misuse of Scripture to blind the masses to their true social circumstances. Blake had made this point several generations earlier, but then his warnings sounded shrill and overstated. It took an industrial revolution, two world wars, and the shock of a nearly triumphant revolutionary atheism to reveal the wisdom in his call for a more socially engaged faith.

Thomas Merton described his own surprising rediscovery of Blake's religious orthodoxy in this passage from *The Seven Storey Mountain*:

> I had imagined that Blake, like the other Romantics, was glorifying passion, natural energy, for their own sake. Far from it! What he was glorifying was the transfiguration of man's natural love, his natural powers, in the refining fires of mystical experience: and that in itself, implied an arduous and total purification, by faith and love and desire, from all the petty materialistic and commonplace and earthly ideals of his rationalistic friends.[10]

Blake's problem with Sir Francis Bacon, John Locke, René Descartes, and Sir Isaac Newton lay in their misappropriation of human reason. Rather than heal the growing disassociation of thought and feeling, they drove a truck though it. Their works make sense only if you buy into the modern delusion of individual metaphysical isolation, duality, and essenceless existence that seals the modern soul in a prison house of the psyche. The new sciences stripped reason of its role as the natural ally of visionary experience—directing the imagination down certain useful materialist paths, rather than allowing it to give birth to unforeseen revelations of divine love.

For Blake, the cosmos was not only a fabric of material objects in space; it had both an inner and an outer reality. When the validity of this inner reality was denied, the creative interplay of mankind with the divine was

10. Thomas Merton, *The Seven Storey Mountain* (New York: Harcourt Brace Jovanovich, 1976), 203.

short-circuited, and we were cut off from the sacred in ourselves and in the world. Thus, modern science constituted both a great leap forward in instrumental knowledge and a second fall from grace. We had become both more powerful and less alive at the same time—more knowing and less content.

The incapacity of the great advocates of progress—Bacon, Newton, Locke, and Descartes—to fathom the tragic nature of these developments only compounded the problem and sent Blake's conservative religious contemporaries in search of new, more rationalist theologies. This, according to Blake, led many believers to betray the gospel's mystic and radical core. And, as a result, it also led to Blake himself being dismissed as a heretic.

Marshall McLuhan described Blake's greatest contribution as explaining for us this shift in Western consciousness from reason as a tool of revelation to reason as an end it itself. Blake's error, he tells us, if that's the word for it, was to use a mythic method in a utilitarian age, and so his peers simply misunderstood his attempt to press back the reactionary phenomenological turn the world was taking. As a result, even his Christian brethren became advocates for the new alienated interior life, reading the Bible in new reductionist and rationalist terms rather than prophetically.

McLuhan remarks:

Blake's diagnosis of the problem of his age was, like Pope's in *The Dunciad,* a direct confrontation of the forces shaping human perception. That he sought mythical form by which to render his vision was both necessary and ineffectual. For myth is the mode of simultaneous awareness of a complex group of causes and effects. In an age of fragmented, lineal awareness, such as produced and was in turn greatly exaggerated by Gutenberg technology, mythological vision remains quite opaque. The Romantic poets fell far short of Blake's mythical or simultaneous vision. They were faithful to Newton's single vision and perfected the picturesque outer landscape as a means of isolating single states of the inner life.[11]

11. Marshall McLuhan, *The Gutenberg Galaxy: The Making of Typographic Man* (Toronto: University of Toronto Press, 1962), 265–66.

In other words, Blake understood that when the spirit loses confidence in itself, the mind falls into the objective world and beings to see creation as something independent. It stops participating with life, stops perceiving beauty and possibility, and, instead, stands in judgment of everything, measuring differences, contrasts, and oppositions. This false objectivity can only be transcended through a return to visionary experience, which alone can restore us to our true, imaginative selves.

The scientific method encourages us to see the world *as a thing outside of our own subjective experience of it.* And once we do that, Blake warned, we start to think that what exists *must necessarily exist*, and that evil and injustice are givens. Such an attitude stifles the flow of human sympathetic awareness and cuts us off from any righteous indignation at the injustices visited upon others. This is why Blake said that a person who is not an artist cannot be a Christian, for the creative imagination is the only vehicle through which love of one's fellow man can be grasped. In Blake's *New Jerusalem* everyone is a visionary and, therefore, everyone experiences the Other as oneself. It is through faith that the primary narcissism of the child is recovered without forfeiting the adult's capacity to discern difference.

The so-called objectivity of time and space clouds our capacity to make this return to the spirit because it replaces the divine cosmos with a world accessible only to our rational minds and breeds an unnecessary identification with our physical bodies as our selves. For Blake, time isn't a real object but the name for three unrealities: a past that doesn't exist any more, a future that never will, and a present that is never quite here. "Space" is only a concept that distinguishes between "here" and "there." It has no real center and no real end. Only the holy immediacy of God within us is present to itself, eternal and always, containing the totality of human existence. But to live in the light of this revelation, one must discount the myriad distinctions and distractions that divide the transcendental unity of the soul-world.

Eternal life is not life that lasts forever; not space-time life going on and on, acquiring more experiences and more things, exhausting itself in the joys of unending stuff. It is, rather, a life free from temporality. Only when we transcend the distinction between subject and object, between here and there, and between now and then, only when we go beyond the concepts of the temporal and the physical, can we begin to understand what holiness truly means. This is why, for the materialists, religious concepts are inherently absurd: they simply cannot accept the possibility that empiricism is a historically conditioned worldview born of the ancient aristocratic desire to control fate and manage history. As a result, they refuse to wake up to Being—remaining unconscious to the eternal and the divine present in each and every experience—preferring instead the heady fantasies of time travel and everlasting cyber-life.

But Blake reminds us again and again that true knowledge—that is to say, knowledge of our ontological status as creatures made in the image of God—cannot be grasped through calculation, only through a *vision*. And *vision*—in its most concentrated and inclusive form—is what psychoanalysts call the "imago," an internal picture that transforms facts into meanings.

Blake's *Milton* and *Jerusalem* express a rethinking of the eschatological meaning of the kingdom of God in response to the reductive, atomist worldview proclaimed by the new sciences. His theme in both these works is that the church lost its radical energy by giving up its apocalyptic vision for a more accommodating set of doctrines, and so the church became more hierarchical and tradition-bound at the very moment it should have become more democratic and imaginative. In this sense, like Milton and Dante before him, and Joyce and Eliot after him, Blake had to create a countermythology to fully express his own understanding of the Christian mysteries as pure revelation. Like the prophets of old, he pointed out how innocence was being swallowed up by worldly experience, and like the apostle Paul, he openly declared the unity of our fallen world with divine eternity.

In this sense, Blake was the first to give us a modern version of the Christian cosmic reversal, which makes him the prototype of many of the figures examined in this book. But his reversal is not the Gnostic theological inversion, nor the heretical counter-Christianity of the "God is Dead" theologians, as Altizer has argued.[12] It is more a reversal of the Christian's relationship to existing society and to the whole idea of incremental moral progress advocated by the new epistemologies. The Enlightenment focus upon objective truth and instrumental reason forced Blake into an adversarial position toward his culture as a whole. Thought and feeling, reason and belief, which had become disassociated in the sixteenth century, had become outright antagonists in the eighteenth. Only by refiguring the prophets and inverting biblical imagery could he find a mode of expression capable of defending the radical revelations of the Christian mythos.

> The Spectre is the Reasoning Power in Man, & when separated
> From Imagination and closing itself as in steel in a Ratio
> Of the Things of Memory, It thence frames Laws & Moralities
> To destroy Imagination, the Divine Body, by Martyrdoms & Wars[13]

Imagination, once an internal faculty, was now governed by the new sciences—each one regulating its expression by the logic of its own, separate, closed system. Prior to this dissociation of sensibility, there was a rough interplay among all of our experiences. To be human was to possess the capacity for expansive and protean awareness. But the entire inner life was now dismissed as fantasy by the laws of scientific inquiry—which replace all our intuitive knowledge with a collection of independent, isolated theories of all the various aspects of the cosmos based upon discipline-specific laws, priests, and hierarchies. Compelled to behold these fragments as the true image of ourselves, we proceeded to destroy systematically whatever remained of our inner lives, which,

---

12. See Thomas J. J. Alitzer's brilliant *The New Apocalypse: The Radical Christian Vision of William Blake* (East Lansing: Michigan State University Press, 1967).
13. William Blake, "Jerusalem," in Blake, *Selected Poetry and Prose*, 302.

in turn, led to a trivialization of the Christian faith as just another out-moded "theory" of man.

The Romantic poets that followed Blake sought a correlative to the inner life in nature, and when that failed, a Gothic revival emerged, using the grotesque as a way to fight the new fragmentation. Baudelaire and the French symbolists followed suit, attempting to dislodge the single vision of modern consciousness, but they were too implicated in the new empiricism and anticlericalism to offer much of an advance.

Blake's insight that the conscious self does not really perceive reality until it recognizes itself as part of what it perceives was frustrated by the fragmentation of the self into the new, diverse, one-dimensional sciences. And so he became a curious but underappreciated outsider whose refusal to accept the first premises of modernity could have helped the "decadents" to bridge the gap between their urban isolation and their lost innocence; perhaps even help them overcome the gap between sin and salvation, dissolving the disassociation of sensibility and thereby ushering in a new visionary epoch.

But that is another story; one that can only be understood by way of Goethe's bold reassessment of the modern mind in the light of his own frustrated longings for a spiritual completion.

Johann Wolfgang von Goethe: Modern Consciousness Explained

> If your heart does not want a world of moral reality, your head will as-suredly never make you believe in one. Mephistophelian skepticism, in-deed, will satisfy the head's play-instincts much better than any rigorous idealism can.
>
> William James, "The Will to Believe"[14]

14. William James, "The Will to Believe," sec. 9 in *The Writings of William James*, ed. John J. McDermott (New York: Random House, 1967), 730.

Although Blake was the first major Western artist to rebel against the reductive rationalism of Newton, Bacon, Locke, and Descartes, Goethe was the first to fully describe the troubled psychology the New Sciences left in their wake. He lived in an age of political consolidation, a time when the nation-states of Europe were gearing up for what would turn out to be massive military confrontations. And yet he saw beyond these worldly maneuverings to the deeper emerging spiritual crisis. He knew that the real story of his time was not the rise and fall of Napoleon, but the rise of Napoleon's unfettered ambitions *in the souls of everyman.* Only a new form of piety could stop this devolution. But this was a hard sell given the modern focus upon demonstrative truth and empirical experimentation, and so Goethe transformed both of these values through a microscopic examination of the metapsychology of the self.

In his breakthrough novella *The Sorrows of Young Werther,* Goethe described the yearnings of a youth out of touch with the emerging new utilitarianism, seeking solace in nature, poetry, love, and self-pity, but not finding it. His desire for spiritual happiness in a world devoid of transcendence leads him to self-pity and ultimately to self-destruction—prefiguring the lives of countless lost adolescents born into a world shedding its religious consolations. The world as a whole moves onward, he told us, but youth must begin ever anew, individually reliving all the epochs of world culture, and therein lies its perpetual value to civilization as a measure of world-self-progress.

Goethe was orthodox only in the sense that he lived in a conventionally Christian culture—accepted its morality, participated in its rituals, and used traditional Christian symbolism in his writing. He himself expressed a variety of views concerning the validity of the Gospels and the divinity of Christ. He even once described institutional Christianity as "an abortive political revolution that turned moral."[15] But his major literary work, *Faust,* remains a textbook expression of orthodox Christianity—pitting the devil against God in a struggle over mankind's immortal soul. Faust

15. Johann Wolfgang von Goethe, *Maxims and Reflections* (New York: Penguin, 1999), 110.

is a representative modern, someone who has mastered the formal disciplines of theology, history, mathematics, and all the other fragmented natural sciences, and yet still longs for integration. He dabbles in the black arts, essentially out of boredom, which puts him into contact with Mephistopheles, who tempts him with the promise of eternal youth and a morally unencumbered life.

Faust's bargain with the devil reflects the spiritual wager of modern man. He doesn't sell his soul, exactly; he merely promises that should he ever feel "content," Mephistopheles can have it. For us moderns this really doesn't constitute much of a risk, for we are relatively certain that there can be no end to our striving. Since there is an infinity of desires to be fulfilled and an infinity of new worlds to conquer, we feel secure in postponing any moral accounting, trusting that at some as yet unforeseen turn in the road, some new insight or breakthrough will open up new options that will make up for all our previous mistakes. An optimistic technocrat and a black arts aficionado, Faust believes, as we do, that the future will justify everything; so "progress" becomes the shibboleth he uses to justify his indifference to the traditional virtues and his faith in the future. What Faust fails to factor into his calculations, however, is the psychological impact the suffering of others will have upon his life. He has bought into the modern dogma of the atomistic self, and Goethe's work exposes the tragedy inherent in buying into this false modern premise.

If you don't remember all the details of the story, Faust seduces and impregnates Margaret, who in turn kills her baby and is executed for her crime. Just before her death, Faust is called to her dungeon from a Walpurgis Night orgy and witnesses her hysterics, her repentance, and ultimately her death. At the very last moment of her life, she repents of her sins and is saved by God's mercy—prefiguring Faust's own salvation in part 2. But at the end of part 1, Faust is left only with the tragic recognition that other people's lives—however much he might want to deny it and however much it may defy reason—do make claims on him. Part 2 ends when Faust experiences the contentment that comes from a moment of selfless love. At that instant, Mephistopheles immediately claims his soul, but Faust repents of his sins, and God redeems him—confirming Goethe's description of Mephistopheles as "part of that power which still produceth good, whilst ever scheming ill."[16]

What is remarkable here is Goethe's insight into the spiritual tragedies inherent both to the Romantic movement, represented by *Werther,* and to the scientific-technological wager represented by *Faust.* These two sides of the modern psyche—its idealistic youthful longings for total personal fulfillment and its cynical midlife thirst for power—serve as two sides of the same cautionary tale. *The Sorrows of Young Werther* warns us not to confuse our desires for reality however authentic they may *feel.* Our dreams can never be fulfilled, because they are a symptom of a deeper longing not of this world. While *Faust* warns us that no matter how much power we have, no matter how infinite our resources, God's providence remains a mystery to our natural selves. These essentially *religious* ideas are more than moral; they are ontological assertions and existential assumptions born of a religious worldview that can be neither proven nor refuted by the scientific method, hence their power as an enduring critique.

It was with the publication of *Wilhelm Meister* that Goethe offered us his solution to these crises. In that novel, the protagonist, Wilhelm, a young man living at the beginning of the second half of the nineteenth century, strives to break free from the restrictive world of economics and to find fulfillment as an actor and playwright. In the course of the novel—the first *Bildungsroman* in world literature—Wilhelm gives expression to a new form of spiritual knowledge that weds religion to life.

Goethe's protagonist meets representatives from all the classes, finally finding his way into an active life of creation through an acceptance and expression of his own inwardness. The artistic life frees him from any dependence upon the German bourgeoisie's political and cultural imperatives. Everything in his life is, thereby, instantly transformed into parable, and he comes to understand that that the greatest mission of the

16. Johann Wolfgang von Goethe, *Faust,* tr. Anna Swanwich (New York: Dove, 1994), 41.

spirit is to elicit the spirit. This becomes his vocation and his salvation from the alienating values of his Enlightenment milieu.

In other words, the inner life, felt as a burden by Werther and as an obstacle to Faust, becomes in *Wilhelm Meister* the very stuff and substance of psychological and spiritual transformation. Wilhelm is, in this sense, the prototype of every subsequent existential hero in world literature, the very model of a soul undeterred by the incomprehension of the world, who embraces his own life's challenges as uniquely ultimate and sacrosanct, even if unseen by the culture at large, outside its categories and its measurement, invisible, incomprehensible, and hidden.

Goethe's novel of development thus became the narrative of the emergence of interiority over and against the world and a lyric expression of consciousness unfolding its reality to itself. One can see its influence everywhere in the works of Fyodor Dostoyevsky, James Joyce, Marcel Proust, Thomas Mann, and Rainer Rilke, but especially in novels of Herman Hesse—whose entire oeuvre is but a footnote to *Wilhelm Meister*.

It was left, however, to Søren Kierkegaard to redirect this modern interior restlessness toward a renewed narrative of Christian salvation.

Kierkegaard: The Transformative Energies of Dread

> The Christianity of Christendom takes away from Christianity the offense, the Paradox, etc., and instead of that introduces probability, the plainly comprehensible. That is, it transforms Christianity into something entirely different from what it is in the New Testament, yea, into exactly the opposite; and this is the Christianity of Christendom, of us men. In the Christianity of Christendom the Cross has become something like the child's hobby-horse and trumpet.
>
> Søren Kierkegaard, "The Instant"[17]

17. Søren Kierkegaard, "The Instant," quoted in the front matter to Jacques Ellul's *The Subversion of Christianity*, trans. Geoffrey W. Bromiley (Grand Rapids: Eerdmans, 1986).

Kierkegaard's whole understanding of man's character is that it is a structure built up to avoid perception of the "terror, perdition [and] annihila-
tion [that] dwell next door to every man." He understood psychology the
way a contemporary psychoanalyst does: that its task is to discover the
strategies that a person uses to avoid anxiety. What style does he use to
function automatically and uncritically in the world, and how does this
style cripple his true growth and freedom of action and choice? Or, in
words that are almost Kierkegaard's: how is a person being enslaved by
his characterological lie about himself?

Ernest Becker, *The Denial of Death*[18]

Goethe's descriptions of the psychology of the modern are deepened
by Kierkegaard's analysis of the dynamics of selfhood. Kierkegaard tells
us that religion continues to exist as a social practice in the modern bourgeois world, but that it now lacks imaginative and intellectual substance.
Modern "Christendom" had become a civil order, given over to various
hypocrisies and biblical pieties, but lacking any authentic relationship
to the Absolute.

In other words, a sense of a centered and coherent self-consciousness
is precisely what individuals lack; therefore, they look around at others,
"the crowd," so that they might pattern themselves after the collective
reality. But all they learn is what the others are. This is how the world
seduces individuals from being themselves. The others, in turn, don't
know who they themselves are, but only who the others are. And so
everyone lives in a house of mirrors, seeking essential life in a world of
appearances and never finding it. Kierkegaard explains:

There is only One who knows what He Himself is and that is God; and
He also knows what every man in himself is, for it is precisely by being
before God that every man has his Being. The man who is not before
God is not himself. A man can be himself only by being before Him who
is in and for Himself. If one is oneself by being in Him who is in and for

18. Ernest Becker, *The Denial of Death* (New York: The Free Press, 1973), 70.

Himself, one can be in others or before others, *but one cannot be oneself being merely before others.*[19]

To the extent that the modern world has become ruled by the crowd, it has become a theater of emptiness and vanity. When we look to each other for a model of Being, the self turns into a Möbius strip, much as the postmodern psychoanalyst Jacques Lacan once described it: a chain of associations, identifications, and existential bluffs. Those who copy conventional "Christian" practices are not really Christians at all, but conformists caught up in the worldly round of mimetic selfhood (see chapter 4). Their souls are empty to the exact degree that they believe they have been "saved" by a formula. The biblical narrative can still call individuals back to a primary relationship to their Creator, but this potential is being lost as its message is made to conform more and more to the psychology of the crowd (that mythic, hypothesized abstraction substantiated via demographics, statistics, and social trends.)

Kierkegaard insisted that in an age of advertising and journalism, rapidly morphing to an age of marketing and propaganda, an individual who tries to find himself in the reflected gaze of another will never know himself. Only religious inwardness, true spiritual solitude, can make possible a different order to life and reveal the inauthenticity of culture itself against the unshakable backdrop of a transcendent God.

We have a feeling of lack, Kierkegaard tells us, because the process of self-creation is an ongoing one. Not until we die will we attain unity with the Absolute. If we could attain this unity here and now, then our desires would be God's desires, and life would not be so confusing. In fact, it would become transparent and divine. But since we are not completed beings, we exist in anxiety, our desires remain arbitrary, and we fall victim to the values of the culture into which we are born. In an attempt to lessen the pain of our anxiety, we take things into our own hands, but this only secures our immature egos against the existential death and rebirth

---

19. Søren Kierkegaard, *Christian Discourses*, trans. Walter Lowrie (Princeton, N.J.: Princeton University Press, 1971), 43. Italics mine.

necessary for our own cultural liberation and spiritual maturity. Sinners find support for their spiritual immaturity by belonging to groups who are immature in the same way; thus, the individual hides in the crowd, which is untruth.

Kierkegaard defined the three styles of human existence: the aesthetic, the ethical, and the religious. The aesthetic is amoral and undogmatic—expressing the joy of being, but fearful of nonbeing, and therefore metaphysically hesitant before the abyss. Ethical individuals recognize something beyond the experiential. They seek to express the radical freedom of individual conscience, the actualization of the inwardness of subjectivity. Their lives constitute a movement toward the infinite interiority of religious experience. But they stop short of its realization, standing back as spectators seeking the true relations of things, fearful of accidental relations, and therefore anxious before the randomness of life, which they attempt to quell through the power of ideology and various other "magical ideas." Religious souls, on the other hand, are conscious of themselves as striving to transform themselves and therefore are suspicious of their own illusory essence. The good they do is not present, but possible, and so they are always somewhat suspicious of their own actions and beliefs and therefore more open to the truth. This is why Kierkegaard claims that "only in despair" can individuals grasp the transient nature of earthly life and become conscious of the reality of the infinite.

Only by accepting one's powerlessness and fallenness, one's dependence on God for an independent and free interior life, can one move beyond the heroic "ethical" defiance of *Faust*. The choice for individuals is, therefore, between defiant persistence in the face of personal despair (existential stoicism) or repentance and submission to true existence in God. This submission, however, is not a form of acquiescence, but the beginning of a purgatorial climb through temporality, suffering, and loss—marked by a decisive but solitary leap into the isolation of faith.

That is to say, once one accepts the absurdity of one's condition and—rather than continue to defy the nonbeing of one's self—decides to side with the Absolute, one finds oneself in opposition to everything aesthetic and ethical. When we see ourselves as we are, dangling over the abyss, indeed inside the abyss—or rather, acknowledging the abyss in us—we realize that we have never really stood anywhere else, and that nothing anyone has every done, said, or achieved can alter this reality.

When this happens, all meanings are reversed, and in the negative image of the judgment we experience mercy. It is in this moment that we understand the meaning of Christ's sacrifice. Made in an instant, the free choice to give up the self produces, as it were, the true self, the authentic person. But it is a choice that must be constantly remade in every subsequent choice, or one falls back into formulas, inauthenticity, and a dependence on the crowd.

This perpetual rechoosing of Christ is the great paradox and challenge of the Christian faith, because the eternal is being perpetually renewed in the temporal. Being is not becoming; it is becoming-again: *beginning*. Choosing Christ is identical with repenting of oneself and marks the transition from an ethical to a religious existence: that simultaneous expression of freedom and necessity in the liberating resignation of love. In his Pulitzer Prize-winning book, *The Denial of Death*, Ernest Becker explains it like this:

> The problem with conventional faith for Kierkegaard is that it can serve as a barrier to one's confrontation with the pure possibility and so substitutes itself for the rebirth of the self necessary for true Christian faith. We must first break through the bounds of our given cultural heroic in order to be open to the true self. By so doing, we link the secret inner self, our authentic talent, our deepest feelings of uniqueness, our inner yearning for absolute significance, to the very ground of creation. Out of the ruins of the broken cultural self there remains the mystery of the private, invisible, inner self which yearns for ultimate significance and cosmic heroism. This invisible mystery at the heart of every creature now attains its cosmic significance by affirming its connection with the invisible mystery at the

heart of creation. This is the meaning of faith. At the same time it is the merger of psychology and religion.[20]

Kierkegaard's great contribution to contemporary thought was to open up serious intellectual inquiry into our personal existence before God. He engaged in an extended anthropological contemplation to map the unknown territory of human spiritual autonomy. In the light of his analyses of the dynamics of faith, Christian Romantics like Blake were revealed as seeking out salvation in a culture that had usurped and trivialized traditional Christian symbols. In attempting to give the Bible back its prophetic power, Blake refigured it into teaching stories, epic images, and prophecies that paralleled the Bible's own revolt against religion.

Goethe was less of a Christian apologist, and more of a spiritual psychologist who understood better than anyone the tragic dynamics of the post-Renaissance mind. The self, freed from its shackles in tradition, prejudice, and superstition, had now become a problem to itself in new and unexpected ways. Untethered from its moorings in any community of faith and set free to roam the interior landscape like a teenage runaway, it was at first fascinated by its own self-discoveries, but soon the new freedom revealed its darker side, and it was left to Kierkegaard to articulate the way back home.

G. K. Chesterton then emerged as the ultimate expression of the turn-of-the-century orthodox avant-garde, arguing for a return to premodern sanity and common sense as an antidote to the emerging new superstitions of progress with their own collection of hoary religious absolutes and superstitions disguised as positivist certainties.

G. K. Chesterton: Preaching to the Converted

Chesterton is not so much great because of his published achievement as great because he is right. His achievement deserves a homage less indis-

20. Becker, *Denial of Death*, 91.

criminate than it has yet been accorded, and that is part of my business in this book; but I do more than praise what he wrote: I praise what he knew. He cannot be praised too highly so long as praise is confined to what is praiseworthy. His especial gift was his metaphysical intuition of being; his especial triumph was his exploitation of paradox to embody that intuition.

Hugh Kenner, *Paradox in Chesterton*[21]

G. K. Chesterton believed that Western civilization was already "Christian" and that Christian values were built into the very warp and woof of every one of its institutional and cultural practices. The problem with the modern West was that many of its best and brightest were trying to cut themselves off from their onto-theological roots while still sitting on the limbs. This generated a howling incommensurability between what the cutting edge thinkers were thinking and the values by which they lived their lives. How can one fight for the equality of all people while at the same time believing in a morally relative universe? Or defend human rights while claiming that moral autonomy is an illusion? The time was ripe for the healing balm of paradox and satire.

Not that one couldn't launch some very good non-Christian explanations to explain these contradictions, but most of them usually raised as many problems as they solved and blamed the confusions on what Nietzsche once described as the "baseless humanitarianism" of the Christian ethos. To expose the internal contradictions inherent in such "modernist" undertakings, Chesterton invoked simple sanity and common sense against the disembodied theorists and dialectical materialists. That is why he saw his calling as "preaching to the converted," for it was the wisdom we already possessed that had become most alien from us.

Most modern Westerners, Chesterton contended, simply don't understand the religious ideas at the heart of their traditions and institutions, and so what they really need is not another revolution (they'd already

21. Hugh Kenner, *Paradox in Chesterton* (New York: Sheed & Ward, 1947), 1.

had several of them) but an honest articulation of how things stood. He wrote:

> We often read nowadays of the valor or audacity with which some rebels attack a hoary tyranny or an antiquated superstition. There is not really any courage at all in attacking hoary or antiquated things, any more than in offering to fight one's grandmother. The really courageous man is he who defies tyrannies young as the morning and superstitions fresh as the first flowers. The only true freethinker is he whose intellect is as free from the future as from the past. He cares as little for what will be as for what has been; he cares only for what ought to be.[22]

"Idolatry is committed," he tells us, "not merely by setting up false gods, but also by setting up false devils; by making men afraid of war or alcohol, or economic law, when they should be afraid of spiritual corruption and cowardice."[23] It is spiritual corruption and vice that lead to the disordering of desires that frustrate our experiences of love and grace and lead us to seek money, power, technique, and prestige. In the throes of these idols of progress, we begin to fear the fights that can set us free and avoid the suffering that will bring us joy.

This is why, Chesterton insists, we need the Scriptures and the teachings of the church. They help us to resist our own impatience with the unpresupposing surfaces of things and pierce our historical ignorance so that we can stop ourselves before we leap into self-defeating revolutions of consciousness, so that we might persist long enough in the faith until the hopelessness of our worldly situation reverses itself in God's own good time. This divine patience is what virtue is and where true revelation comes from. This long endurance in the good is not only a religious value; it's a characterological absolute, and all the virtues are contained within it.

---

22. G. K. Chesterton, *What's Wrong with the World* (London: Cassell, 1910), 32–33.
23. G. K. Chesterton, *Illustrated London News*, September 11, 1909.

Chesterton believed that modern civilization was producing things faster than we could think or give thanks.[24] He thus set out to show how a more just "distribution" of capital could give expression of biblical values and point us toward a more just and equitable economic system. "Distributism," as this view was called, also championed by the Catholic writer Hilaire Belloc, held that private property was a good thing provided it was fairly *distributed*. It stakes out a middle ground between both communist and capitalist excesses.

Chesterton argued that we don't need a socialist state so much as we need more independently owned farms and businesses. The problem with capitalism was that it wasn't really capitalism; it was corporate socialism. Fewer families were owning more and more of the means of production and using government to protect their interests. The solution to this inequality was not communism—which would only further disenfranchise the workers in the name of that vacuous abstraction "the people." Nor was it "less government," for that would help only those already rich. Rather, the answer was decentralization and greater distribution of the means of production. "There cannot be a nation of millionaires," Chesterton contended, "and there never has been a nation of Utopian comrades; but there have been any number of nations of tolerably contented peasants."[25]

If capital were owned by as many families as possible, wealth would be allocated more reasonably and those who most needed help would be assured of finding it. "The modern city is ugly," Chesterton wrote, "not because it is a city but because it is not enough of a city, because it is a jungle, because it is confused and anarchic, and surging with selfish and materialistic energies."[26] Likewise, capitalism was failing, not because it was capitalistic, but because it wasn't capitalistic enough.

24. G. K. Chesterton, *Daily News*, February 21, 1902.

25. G. K. Chesterton, *Outline of Sanity* (London: Methuen, 1928), 192.

26. G. K. Chesterton, *Lunacy and Letters,* ed. Dorothy Collins (London and New York: Sheed & Ward, 1958), 78.

Everything, Chesterton noted, was upside-down. The Anarchists called themselves democrats when they were really totalitarians. The literary avant-garde called itself revolutionary when it was really reactionary. The capitalists claimed to value free markets when what they really wanted was control over the markets. Only a perspective not of this world, independent of history, time, and contemporary politics, had any chance of describing things correctly. And for Chesterton that perspective was best provided by orthodox Christian faith that—contrary to its modernist critics—was neither narrowly dogmatic nor doctrinally frozen, but—when properly understood—morally self-critical and politically liberating.

Chesterton remarked that "Marxism will in a generation or so go into the limbo of most heresies, but meanwhile it will have poisoned the Russian Revolution."[27] He had no quarrel with the peasants and workers taking control of their own destiny, but once their self-determination was hijacked by a tiny ideological faction, it ceased to be either progressive or ethical. "You can never have a revolution in order to establish a democracy," he pointed out. "You must have a democracy in order to have a revolution."[28] Social critics, he contended, should direct their energies not toward destroying bourgeois institutions, but rather at increasing democratic participation in those institutions and laying bare the onto-theological basis of the culture at large.

Perhaps no one understood this better than the disillusioned Marxist Nikolai Berdyaev, who set out to refurbish the social meaning of Christian revelation from the inside out.

Nikolai Berdyaev: The Death of the Spirit in the Birth of the Bottom Line

The past generation was able to live in intellectual positivism because it was educated in Christian faith; it carried this faith beneath its positivism,

27. G. K. Chesterton, *Illustrated London News*, July 19, 1919.
28. G. K. Chesterton, *Tremendous Trifles* (London: Methuen, 1909), 74.

as its unconscious support. But a generation educated in positivism must return by force to seek the hidden spring which its parents closed for it.

Miguel de Unamuno, *Cartas Inéditas*[29]

Nikolai Berdyaev was one of those late-nineteenth-century progressive Russian theocrats who became disillusioned with Marxism after the Bolsheviks threw him into prison. He then returned to his Christian faith with a new energy, commitment, and resolve—developing most of his innovative ideas while living in exile in Paris, where he died in 1948.

Berdyaev was orthodox in his Christocentric theology but avant-garde in his existential critiques of both Marxism and the new bourgeoisie: orthodox in his admiration of the Christianity of Dostoyevsky, Soloviev, and Tolstoy but avant-garde in his application of their ideas to Russian literature and art. He was orthodox in his use of Christian categories to launch moralistic critiques of contemporary thinkers and social trends, but avant-garde in his apocalyptic reading of history and in his rejection of moral gradualism and material progress.

For him the word *bourgeois* meant more than just middle class: it was a state of the soul characterized by a degrading clutching after security and a small-mindedness incapable of imagining a world much larger than one's own. The bourgeois didn't worship money per se, but they were addicted to personal success, security, and happiness. For these things, they willingly compromised their honor, ignored injustice, and betrayed truth, replacing these high values with trite moralisms and facile bromides that blurred important distinctions and justified selfish actions. Gone were the aristocratic intangibles and noblesse oblige; in came certainty, self-promotion, and moxie.

The "bourgeois," in other words, was an idolater proud of his idolatry, and although the bourgeois spirit had always existed, Berdyaev believed that it reached its peak in the late nineteenth century, when the desire for affluence triumphed over any residual aspiration for holiness, greatness,

---

29. Miguel de Unamuno, *Carta inéditas,* quoted in Daniel Murphy, *Christianity and Modern European Literature* (Dublin; Portland, Oreg.: Four Courts Press, 1997), 131.

or genius.[30] This moral debasement of world civilization continued into the twentieth century, with the middle class gaining such power and influence that the word *bourgeois* became synonymous with mean-spirited wealth, narrow-minded technological know-how, and a preoccupation with worldly success. The cultural ideals of the knight, the monk, the philosopher, and the poet were all superseded by the cultural ideal of the businessman. The will to power had been usurped by the "will to well-being." Berdyaev remarks:

> A religion of progress based on this apotheosis of a future fortunate generation is without compassion for either present or past; it addresses itself with infinite optimism to the future, with infinite pessimism to the past. It is profoundly hostile to the Christian expectation of resurrection for all mankind, for all the dead, fathers and forefathers. This Christian idea rests on the hope of an end to historical tragedy and contradiction valid for all human generations, and of resurrection in eternal life for all who have ever lived.[31]

The bourgeois did not repudiate religion but reinterpreted its value in terms of utility. The love of the poor moved to the periphery of the faith and was embraced only insofar as it didn't clash with one's own personal economic interests. This inversion of means and ends—so central also to Matthew Arnold's critique of the modern Philistines in *Culture and Anarchy*—signaled, for Berdyaev, the death of the spirit in the birth of the bottom line. He wrote:

> The perfected European and American civilizations gave rise to the industrial-capitalist system, which represents not only a mighty economic development *but the spiritual phenomenon of the annihilation of spirituality*. The industrial Capitalism of civilization proved to be the destroyer

30. Ibid.

31. Nikolai Berdyaev, *The Meaning of History*, trans. George Reavey (Cleveland: Meridian Books, 1962 [1936]), quoted in "Nicholas Berdyaev, Prophet for the Catholic Worker Movement," in *The Houston Catholic Worker* 15, no. 4 (May–June 1995).

of the eternal spirit and sacred traditions. Modern capitalist civilization is essentially atheistic and hostile to the idea of God. The crime of killing God must be laid at its door rather than at that of revolutionary socialism, which merely adapted itself to the civilized "bourgeois" spirit and accepted its negative heritage.[32]

This may seem like blasphemy to modern free-marketers who think of themselves as "Christians," but for Berdyaev anything that put material development before the kingdom of God was suspect. It was not enough to pursue material gain six days out of the week and holiness on Sundays. The bourgeois was not really hypocritical; they knew what they were doing. It was just that they forgave themselves too easily and justified their avarice as a form of pragmatic realism—just as Blake had predicted they would. The materialism of Descartes, Locke, and Newton had replaced the invisible God of transcendence with the God of progress and commerce.

Berdyaev explains:

Civilization, as opposed to culture, which is given up to the contemplation of eternity, tends to be futurist. Machinery and technique are chiefly responsible for the speeding up of life and its exclusive aspiration towards the future. Organic life is slower, less impetuous, and more concerned with essentials, while civilized life is superficial and accidental; for it puts the means and the instruments of life before the ends whose significance is lost. The consciousness of civilized men is concentrated exclusively upon the means and techniques of life considered as the only reality, while its aims are regarded as illusory.[33]

To Berdyaev, commercial life is anti-contemplative and, therefore, anti-spiritual; it is essentially futurist in its subjection of the eternal to the temporal, the spiritual to the material, and the present to the future.

32. Ibid. Italics mine.
33. Ibid.

Nothing is of value in and of itself; everything is fodder for economic development, social change, technological growth, and industrial productivity. Even leisure and rest are valued for what they add to one's productivity. Time is money, and money power.

This view of time as a commodity—indeed of life, spirit, health, and meaning as commodities—creates a new human type focused upon personal achievement. Again, Berdyaev remarks:

> As a reaction against the medieval ascetic ideal, man puts aside both resignation and contemplation, and attempts to dominate nature, organize life and increase its productive forces. This, however, does not help to bring him into closer communion with the inner life and soul of nature. On the contrary, by mastering it technically and organizing its forces man becomes further removed from it. Organization proves to be the death of the organism. Life becomes increasingly a matter of technique. The machine sets its stamp upon the human spirit and all its manifestations. Thus civilization has neither a natural nor a spiritual, but a mechanical foundation. It represents par excellence the triumph of technique over both the spirit and the organism.[34]

A vicious cycle ensues: the machine society reinforces the bourgeois self, which in turn seeks greater control over nature, thereby distancing itself even further from any ascetic ideals.

The existential freedom created by God, Berdyaev insists, has an altogether different source from this bourgeois freedom to turn one's life into a thing. God's freedom is not expressed through our reason, our accomplishments, or even our experiences. It expresses not only what is in our power but also what lies outside it. It is the freedom Dostoyevsky talks about when he argues that the purpose of life is to prove to ourselves at every moment of our existence that we are not "piano keys" but free souls, even if we are not! This radical spiritual freedom comes to us from faith, which puts an end to our fear that we do not matter, that we

34. Ibid.

are merely playthings of the fates, and that our lives make sense only in terms of social values and economic success.

For Berdyaev, any identification of the abstract patterns and cycles of history with divinity is blasphemy. The mystery of "grace" transcends, reconciles, and resolves the clash between freedom and necessity, fate and providence, the collective and the individual. This is why life is tragic and civilization cyclical. We are not moving toward utopia; we are condemned to be free. But if we can acknowledge our helplessness and sinful nature, it is possible to transcend ourselves in God's free gift of grace.

As a reborn Russian Orthodox, Berdyaev took a second look at world history through the lens of Marxism and saw not only Hegel turned on his head, but a world on fire. Victimized himself by Bolshevik ideals and pretensions, he preferred the holy apocalypse of Saint John to Lenin's bloody revolution and looked again into the Book of Revelation for inspiration. What he found there was a completely different way of looking at the world: poetic, visionary, and eschatological—the point of view of the individual soul in eternity, not the perspective of a dying egoistic self looking through the haze of human projects, goals, and failed agendas. This vision of a world redeemed struck him by its liberating ordering of life's particulars and its engagement with the horrors of time and change. In the light of such a vision, human existence could not be reduced to the search for security; the real fight was elsewhere: in that hidden sphere known intimately only to mystics, saints, and heroes, where death stands unappeased by our accomplishments and we transcend death in our brave defiance of time.

It is this sphere of existence that the great modern novelists spend their entire lives exploring.

2

The Novel as Countermythology

The only philosophy which can be responsibly practiced in the face of despair is the attempt to contemplate all things as they would present themselves from the standpoint of redemption. Knowledge has no light but that shed on the world by redemption: all else is reconstruction, mere technique. Perspectives must be fashioned that displace and estrange the world, reveal it to be, with all its rifts and crevices, as indigent and distorted as it will appear one day in the messianic light. To gain such perspectives without velleity or violence, entirely from felt contact with its objects—this alone is the task of thought.

Theodore Adorno, *Minima Moralia*[1]

It is true that storytelling reveals meaning without committing the error of defining it, that it brings about content and reconciliation with things as they really are, and that we

1. Theodore Adorno, "Finale," from *Minima Moralia* (Frankfurt: Suhrkamp, 1951), 247.

may even trust it to contain eventually by implication that
last word which we expect from the "day of judgment."

Hannah Arendt, *Men in Dark Times*[2]

Everything and especially philosophy is
strictly speaking novel or legend.

Miguel de Unamuno[3]

The novel's wisdom is different from that of philosophy. The
novel is born not of the theoretical spirit but of the spirit of
humor. One of Europe's major failures is that it never under-
stood the most European of the arts—the novel; neither its spirit,
nor its great knowledge and discoveries, nor the autonomy of
its history. The art inspired by God's laughter does not by na-
ture serve ideological certitudes, it contradicts them. Like Pe-
nelope, it undoes each night the tapestry that the theologians,
philosophers, and learned men have woven the day before.

Milan Kundera, *The Art of the Novel*[4]

Only in the context of a renewed appreciation for the power of myth does the contemporary religious imagination begin to revive. Not because we have drifted back into a premodern irrationality, but because we have moved forward into an information-saturated, multidimensional, multidisciplinary mediated environment of the whole—into a world so dense with significance that only literature can penetrate it. Myth and poetry, as it turns out, far from being antiquated forms, happen to be the fastest and most information-laden methods of modern communication: the very best means by which existential existence and reason can be conjoined into a single, unified expression.

2. Hannah Arendt, *Men in Dark Times* (New York: Harcourt Brace Jovanovich, 1970), 105.
3. Quoted in Murphy, *Christianity and Modern European Literature,* 136.
4. Milan Kundera, *The Art of the Novel,* trans. Linda Asher (New York: Perennial Library, 1988), 160.

The novel, as a genre, was born into this age as the narrative of consciousness. The inner life no longer fit its outer circumstances, and the novel told the story of the soul's attempt to close the gap: either by living in dreams, giving up its interior life entirely, or negotiating some tragicomic compromise with existence itself. The Hungarian critic Georg Lukacs described it as the "epic of homelessness" and considered Cervantes' story of an idealist lost in a realist world, *Don Quixote,* its signature work and urtext: a human being lost among commodities and social roles seeking beauty, truth, and justice became the master plot and template for virtually every novel written after it.

The Czech novelist Milan Kundera describes the novel as the place existential thought migrated after philosophy was taken over by the positivists—preserving reflection in an age driven by ideological abstractions. In his essay "The Depreciated Legacy of Cervantes," Kundera wrote:

> If it is true that philosophy and science have forgotten about man's being, it emerges all the more plainly that with Cervantes a great European art took shape that is nothing other than the investigation of this forgotten being. Indeed, all the great existential themes Heidegger analyzes in *Being and Time*—considering them to have been neglected by all earlier European philosophy—have been unveiled, displayed, illuminated by four centuries [four centuries of European reincarnation of the novel]. In its own way, through its own logic, the novel discovered the various dimensions of existence one by one.[5]

As such, the novel has been the primary vehicle for spiritual reflection in the West throughout the modern era. The theologians in their conversation with the scientists and philosophers have simply taken the wrong road home.

How could they not have seen that the concerns of the novel are the same as those of religion? And that even though a novelist might be an atheist or a materialist, the genre itself demands a focus upon the concrete

5. Ibid., 4, 5.

over the abstract, the incarnational over the merely theoretical, and the synthesis of character, thought, and action in the person rather than in a "theory of man." Narrative form, as it turns out, is inherently eschatological, logocentric, humanist, and humane.

And yet, the metaphysical basis of the novel in Western Christianity is treated as an embarrassment or a scandal—even by religious literary critics. Consideration of the Christian contribution to the modern novel are either limited to reflections on books by Graham Greene, Evelyn Waugh, and Flannery O'Connor or denounced by Derridian poststructuralists.

But the novel was never the vehicle for ideology or Christian apologetics so much as the great countermythological genre, an essential expression of "felt" modern experience at war with the mythological framework that created it. Or, another way of saying this is that the novel was born at that very moment when experience itself was being transformed by commerce and politics. Its primary concerns are with the lost soul's pilgrimage on earth, the clash of the ideal with the real, the fallen with the saved, naturalism with idealism, and the myth of transcendence with the experience of quotidian reality.

From Cervantes, Fielding, Dickens, and Balzac all the way up to Dostoyevsky's dialogic narratives, James Joyce's secular epiphanies,[6] and Walker Percy's forays into postmodern semiotic cosmogony, spiritual concerns have fueled the form, and the form itself has interrogated its own Christian sources. As a result, novelists may be our truest theologians of the modern—the first and finest flowering of the Christian orthodox avant-garde.

---

6. For a profound but largely overlooked reading of Joyce as a modern Christian visionary, see Marshall McLuhan, *The Medium and the Light: Reflections of Religion*, ed. Eric McLuhan and Jacek Szklarek (Toronto: Stoddart, 1999), 172–74: "What Joyce is saying is that for the first time in history many now have the means of observing the social process as the process of redemption. This he can do because the social process is the analogue of the process of sense perception and interior cognition. And the process of perception is that of incarnation. . . . For anybody concerned with the subject of Catholic humanism in modern letters I should think that Joyce's insight, which was marvelously realized in his work, is the most inspiriting development that is possible to conceive. But we must ask, what happens when this insight occurs even in a fragmentary way to the secular minds of our age?"

Dostoyevsky's Dharma: On the Origins of Christian Modernism

Dostoyevsky did not write novels, and the creative vision revealed in his works has nothing to do, either as affirmation or as rejection, with European nineteenth-century Romanticism or with the many, likewise Romantic, reactions against it. He belongs to the new world. Only formal analysis of his works can show whether he is already the Homer or the Dante of that world or whether he merely supplies the songs which, together with the songs of other great forerunners, later artists will one day weave into a great unity: whether he is merely a beginning or already a completion. It will then be the task of historio-philosophical interpretation to decide whether we are really about to leave the age of absolute sinfulness or whether the new has no other herald but our hopes: those hopes which are signs of a world to come, still so weak that it can easily be crushed by the sterile power of the merely existent.

Georg Lukacs, The Theory of the Novel[7]

Most literary scholars agree that Dostoyevsky reinvented the modern novel as a unique philosophical genre: a form of thought-in-motion, life-in-thought, fiction as spiritual experiment—and thereby changed the way we read all narratives, including the Bible. And yet Dostoyevsky's love of the novel—tempered by his even more intense love of Christ—tells a slightly different story: the story of a deeply orthodox religious conscience finding in the novel a mode of expression capable of questioning the role of European values in Russian culture. His art was the expression of his own tortured search for redemption, serving both as a means of discovery and as an instrument for self-transformation.

Consequently, his literary legacy is vast, troubled, and distorted. He is often praised for the wrong virtues, criticized for the wrong faults, and misunderstood by those who most need to hear what he has to say. He is celebrated as a modernist, doubter, and skeptic, criticized for his "lapses"

---

7. George Lukacs, *The Theory of the Novel*, trans. Anna Bostock (Cambridge: MIT Press, 1971), 152–53.

into Christian apologetics, and appropriated by the very fanatics and intellectual snobs he strove his entire life to expose as frauds.

Most of his novels are not great works but flawed, moral/aesthetic experiments—heroic attempts to solve insoluable problems: to reconcile Christianity with Enlightenment skepticism, faith with doubt, and terror with hope. And most of them fail. René Girard (see chapter 4) even goes so far as to say that "Dostoyevsky and his work are exemplary, not in the sense of a corpus of work and a life without fault, but in exactly the opposite sense. In observing this author live and write we learn, perhaps, that peace of soul is the most difficult of conquests and that genius is not a natural phenomenon."[8]

Dostoyevsky wrote many drafts and revised endlessly. And although much of what he wrote had the mark of genius, it was never flawless. His last book, *The Brothers Karamazov,* brought all the partial successes together into one great crowning achievement—revealing all that went before as steps in a single all-encompassing spiritual progression. Albert Einstein once described *The Brothers Karamazov* as the greatest book ever written. Herman Hesse said that European and especially German youth were destined to find their greatest writer in Dostoyevsky—not in Goethe.[9] T. E. Lawrence insisted that *The Brothers Karamazov* constituted a "Fifth Gospel," bringing the radical vision of the New Testament into dialogue with the realities of the modern age.

Dostoyevsky's own remarks confirm these assessments. He said that he'd had to pass through a great "furnace of doubt" before he could finish the novel—passing though every modern illusion to finally arrive at a faith beyond faith. *The Brothers Karamazov,* in this sense, documents Dostoyevsky's journey through European nihilism to a second innocence. As such, it is the single most significant work of spiritual direction written in the modern era, and at the same time, perhaps, the single most telling

8. René Girard, *Resurrection from the Underground,* trans. James G. Williams (New York: Cross-road, 1997), 14.

9. From "The Brothers Karamazov, or the End of Europe," in *In Sight of Chaos,* trans. Stephen Hudson (Zurich: Verlag Selduyla, 1923), 13–21.

critique of conventional religious piety ever composed. He accomplished this, in part, by the supra-Realist aesthetics he employed—embracing all life's failures and misdeeds with the same energy, joy, and love with which he accepted everything else: his shame as well as his accomplishments, the awful truth about life as well as its beauty.

Dostoyevsky is orthodox in his desire to write apologetics, but avant-garde in his unflinching attempt to disclose the psychological dynamics of the underground. Orthodox in his attempt to describe the perfect Christian, but avant-garde in his experiments in polyphonic narrative form and in his attempt to synthesize the wisdom of Jesus, Buddha, and Balzac within a single imaginative vision. Orthodox in his own search for spiritual guidance from the Staretz, but avant-garde in his dialogic rendering of that advice. Orthodox in his description of Zossima and Alyosha—avant-garde in his rendering of Dimitri and the Grand Inquisitor.

His first attempt at articulating Christian virtue—*The Idiot*—failed to achieve these ends. The romantic faith of Prince Myshkin embodies a kind of orthodox quixotism and thus could not, in the end, pass the test of the novel form. That is to say, the beauty and truth of his character could not be rendered convincingly as a "possible life." Dostoyevsky was too honest an artist and too sincere a human being to slant his fictions to fit his own religious beliefs. The novel, by his own admission, actually demonstrates the opposite of what he wanted to achieve: rather than show the power of Christian faith to overcome modern Philistinism, it actually demonstrates its tragic impotence before it.

It wasn't until he wrote *The Brothers Karamazov* that Dostoyevsky was able to compose a narrative Christian apologetics that worked. In that novel every conceivable alternative point of view had to be countered and qualified—not only by its opposites, but also by its asymmetrical complements, its half-measures, and its shadow sides. If he presented a character who embraced Christianity, he felt obliged to present an equally attractive character who rejected it. Not only that, he also felt the need to present lower- and higher-order skeptics and a lower- and higher-order people of faith to set them off. Then he would dramatize misapprehending critics and supporters of all three in order to separate even more accurately the real skeptics and believers from the various inauthentic ciphers impersonating them.

In other words, as much as he wanted his novel to give testimony to the Christian faith, he also believed an artist must play fair. Thus, he couldn't bend reality to fit his character's needs. As a result, his sinners are as profound as his saints, his skeptics as moral as his believers; and his take on what is wrong with the modern world turned out also to reveal what was wrong with the traditional one.

In this sense *The Brothers Karamazov* is not a work of Christian apologetics in the traditional sense of that term, but rather the expression of its author's own struggle to realize the true meaning of his faith, a working through—not philosophically or logically but imaginatively—of what it means to practice active love, what it means to turn suffering into happiness, and what it means to die so that you may be reborn. It is the story of Alyosha's attainment of what Paul Tillich called "the courage to be," how he absorbs into his being the maximum amount of non-being, thereby achieving the maximum amount of human authenticity. What Dostoyevsky is describing in Alyosha "is not a creature who is transformed and who transforms the world in turn in some miraculous ways, but rather a creature who takes more of the world into himself and develops new forms of courage and endurance."[10]

This is not a particularly new project for a writer; it is as old as Homer and as young as Shakespeare. But the modern world within which Alyosha's development takes place, and the Christian vision that informs it, makes *The Brothers Karamazov* the first full and successful articulation of Christian modernism (and the ultimate expression of what I am calling here the orthodox avant-garde). In Alyosha, Dostoyevsky finds a convincing champion of the faith who is neither a quixotic fool nor a tragic victim—but a living synthesis of Western realism and Eastern

10. Becker, *Denial of Death*, 279.

mysticism. The book lampoons cheap grace, explores the darkest depths of philosophical nihilism, and takes a hard look at sexual fetishes, sadomasochism, dysfunctional family relationships, totalitarianism, and bogus religiosity.

Unfortunately, the text's status as a book of modern spiritual direction has been lost on recent scholarship. As brilliant as Bakhtin's analysis of Dostoyevsky's dialogic poetics is—and I think it remains the most thought-provoking of all the theoretical commentaries on Dostoyevsky's work—it does not address the spiritual needs of today's reader. And yet I can think of no other work—except, perhaps, Bonhoeffer's *Letters from Prison*—that so accurately diagnoses the spiritual crises of our age or penetrates to the very essence of our moral blindnesses and self-destructive urges.

Dostoyevsky discovered in the prison camps that human beings prefer to exercise their will over their reason, that they are at bottom irrational, driven not by self-interest, but by an insatiable desire *to matter,* to leave their mark, to be heard—even if all they say is a curse. Joseph Frank, Dostoyevsky's biographer, explained that he

> did not portray these precepts (the fundamental irrationality of man) merely as guides to ordinary social behavior; for him they raised profound moral-philosophical questions far transcending their sources in the material on which he drew, and he traced them back to their nihilistic roots in the clash between the fundamental principles of Judeo-Christian morality and the secular alternatives offered by Nihilism. It is this imaginative capacity to raise the social to the tragic, combined with his psychological genius, that gives his greatest works such universal scope and still undiminished power.[11]

On the surface *The Brothers Karamazov* is a saint's life. The book presents us with a Christian apostle confronting the realities of modern life, and

11. Joseph Frank, *Dostoevsky: The Miraculous Years, 1865–1871* (Princeton, N.J.: Princeton University Press, 1995), 7.

although he doesn't exactly triumph over them, he does something even more significant: he abandons himself to divine providence, and by so doing allows those experiences to perfect his character. As the novel progresses Alyosha's way becomes clearer and more and more defined. He models Christian faith as a way of life: it doesn't do away with life's paradoxes; it actually enlarges them. But by demonstrating Christ's radical ethic of perpetual inward renewal, Alyosha models for us the full meaning of Dostoyevsky's epigram "Without suffering, happiness cannot be understood."

The novel is polyphonic in the sense that every event "comments" on some other event. There are many voices and antitheses—a saint for every sinner—a moment of blasphemy for every moment of sublimity. These contrasts generate a vast literary grammar that evolves throughout the text, deepening all that follows in an ever-increasing explication of the human condition as an experience of sustained becoming.

The story is not just a story of brothers struggling to redeem a corrupt patriarchy or religious hope fighting against intellectual despair. It is also the story of how the human soul devours its world—how the hunger for life works—how it is that the good die young, the suicide dies with a smile on his lips, and the bravest and brightest among us find themselves alone in a room with a dimestore devil debating the finer points of epistemology. In a letter to his brother, Dostoyevsky himself tried to explain his achievement:

> I alone traced the tragedy of the underground, which consists in suffering, in self-punishment, in the awareness of something better, and the impossibility of attaining it—above all in the clear conviction of these unhappy people that everyone is the same as they are and so there's no point in trying to reform! What could support those who tried to reform? Reward? Faith? There is no one to give rewards, no one to believe in. One step further and we have extreme depravity, crime (murder). The cause of the underground is the destruction of faith in general rules. There is nothing sacred.[12]

12. Quoted by Donald Fanger in his introduction to Fyodor Dostoyevsky, *Notes from Underground* (New York: Bantam Classic, 1989), xxv.

But the cure to the psychology of the underground is as surprising as it is profound: we are not quite what we imagine ourselves to be, nor are we quite as in control of our beliefs as we think, not quite so essential as we imagine. Our loves and identities move in and through us like viral infections. And yet hope stands before us in places we never suspected: the moment more complex than an eternity, and faith different altogether than anything we now know. To love one another in this world requires us to endure the opaque fog of history, to look past the ghosts of our ambitions, to carry the cross of our own distorted, particular lives.

In the introduction to *The Brothers Karamazov,* Dostoyevsky tells us that Alyosha is the protagonist of the book; that this is, in fact, the first volume of a two-volume work; and that his principle goal as a writer is to make the heroism of this simple, good man apparent to his readers. The modern world, he admits, respects the wicked more than the virtuous and for some very good reasons. Vital amorality really is a positive advance over the soft-headed and thick-skinned conformity of the European bourgeois. And so to invent a hero who is *not wicked* requires a double movement: first, to expose the self-defeating logic inherent in the wicked man's strategy of rebellion; and second, to demonstrate the continuing relevance of traditional religious virtues.

Alyosha does not aspire to move *beyond* good and evil but positions himself between them—on the cross. This is Alyosha's way: through the acceptance of his limitations, his vulnerability, his powerlessness, and his need for grace, he ceases to identify with his own personal problems and reidentifies with God's suffering in the world. In this sense *The Brothers Karamazov* is not a saint's story proper, because Alyosha is not strictly speaking "a sign from God." But he is on the way to becoming one. And the book provides us with a set of lessons documenting this transformation as Alyosha learns how to face up to the contradictions of the real world. That is to say, he takes into himself an ever greater share of the problematics of life. He doesn't wall himself off in isolation or flee internally to some intellectual safe house; he embraces complexity and nonbeing. As a result, his daily life becomes a duty of cosmic proportions, and he becomes an anticipatory being, a prototype rather than an archetype.

Dostoyevsky is setting out to forge in the smithy of Alyosha's soul the uncreated conscience of his race. And like Stephen Dedalus, his vocation is that of an artist—not that of a priest—destined to learn his own wisdom apart from others or "to learn the wisdom of others himself, wandering among the snares of the world."[13] In a very moving passage, Joyce describes the young artist walking down the lane as the faint sour stink of rotted cabbages come towards him from the kitchen gardens on the rising ground above the river, and he smiles to think "that it is this disorder, the misrule and confusion of his father's house and the stagnation of vegetable life, which was to win the day in his soul."[14] It is at this moment that Stephen, like Alyosha, sets out "to live, to err, to fall, to triumph, to recreate life out of life."[15]

It is no accident that Stephen's affirmation of stinky cabbages parallels Alyosha's affirmation of Zossima's stinking corpse. In that moment of awakening when Alyosha leaves the church with Zossima's rapidly decomposing body inside, and he realizes the full meaning of Zossima's advice to him—to leave the monastery and enter the world, to love the earth, and the animals, and the people. He throws himself down onto the ground to embrace the dust of reality. "He fell to the earth a weak youth," Dostoyevsky tells us, "but he arose a resolute champion."[16]

Alyosha is now capable of abandoning himself to divine providence—not in the passive sense of taking whatever life gives him, but in the prophetic sense of accepting life's difficulties and imperfections as the very stuff of his destiny. Nothing must be rejected, but everything accepted from God's hand. This is what Zossima meant when he told him that in his sorrows he was to find his happiness.

13. James Joyce, *Portrait of the Artist as a Young Man* (New York: Penguin, 2003 [1910]), 158.
14. Ibid.
15. Ibid., 168.
16. Fyodor Dostoyevsky, *The Brothers Karamazov*, trans. Constance Garnett (New York, London: W. W. Norton, 1976 [1881]), 341.

Dostoyevsky seems to be arguing here that if the work of sanctifica-tion seems to present us with insurmountable difficulties, it is because we do not know how to form a just idea of it. In essence, sanctity is simply fidelity to the duties appointed by God. In Alyosha's case these duties present themselves in the form of daily crises: everything from the trial of his murderous brother to the psychodramas of his sado-masochistic fiancée. But through these struggles, God teaches him not to fear nonbeing but to ingest it as a kind of spiritual food, for it is only by undergoing mortifications, by trials and deprivations of all kinds, that he learns how to overcome his self-defeating preoccupation with the ephemeral.

If there is any heresy here, it's that Alyosha does not live in joyful expectation of the coming of the Lord so much as inside the perpetual realization that life has already been redeemed. And so, the choice is his as to whether he will realize God's love in the moment by seizing upon one of its as yet unrealized possibilities or pass it by. The fact that such transforming realizations are so seldom chosen does not lead this saint to despair, but rather confirms him in his vocation to lift those caught in the psychology of the underground back up into the light.

The Dostoyevskian saint says "let the worst come." By unburdening himself from goals and expectations and embracing poverty, solitude, and obedience, he liberates himself from fear while at the same time opening himself up to a whole, hitherto unrecognized, field of existential discovery. It is here one begins to experience that "interpenetration of worlds" Zossima talks about.

This transcendent and transformative perspective on existence sur-vived the Russian Revolution in the form of an underground literary resistance spearheaded by Boris Pasternak—culminating in Alek-sandr Solzhenitsyn's world-shattering experimental novel *The Gulag Archipelago*.

Redeeming Dissidents: Boris Pasternak and Aleksandr Solzhenitsyn

> Pasternak's Christianity is something very simple, very rudimentary, deeply sincere, utterly personal and yet for all its questionable expressions, obviously impregnated with the true spirit of the Gospels and the Liturgy.
>
> Thomas Merton, *Literary Essays*[17]

> Mayakovsky acts upon us, Pasternak within us. Pasternak isn't read by us: he takes place in us.
>
> Marina Tsvetaeva, *Art in the Light of Conscience*[18]

Boris Pasternak once described himself as an atheist who had lost his faith in atheism. Born Jewish, he was brought up by his nanny in the Russian Orthodox faith. But as a young man he became a skeptic and supported the October Revolution as Russia's best chance to turn the tables on history and right the wrongs of its tyrannical past. When the revolution turned sour and its idealism was betrayed, Pasternak lost his faith in faithlessness and became an "internal émigré" living in quiet protest against the new totalitarian state, quietly translating *Hamlet* and *Faust* and, along with Anna Akhmatova, Marina Tsvetaeva, and Mandelstam, launching a radical defense of the poetic imagination through clandestine readings and private publications that would reverberate throughout the world as one of greatest defenses of conscience in all of literary history.

During this time of persecution, he tells us, he "came to understand the Bible, not so much as a book with a hard and fast text as the notebook of humanity and a key to everything that is eternal."[19] Although there was no chance that Pasternak's dissident works would be published by the

---

17. Thomas Merton, *Literary Essays* (New York: New Directions, 1981), 43.

18. Marina Tsvetaeva, *Art in the Light of Conscience,* trans. Angela Livingstone (Cambridge: Harvard University Press, 1992), 109.

19. Boris Pasternak, *Safe Conduct,* quoted in *Pasternak: Prose & Poems,* ed. Stefan Schimanski (London: E. Benn, 1959), 87.

party-controlled press, he continued to write about the struggles of his life and those of his countrymen under Stalin, often passing his poems on by word of mouth, since a written record could be dangerous to both the poet and the reader.

Pasternak captured the quiet courage of his fellow poets in his poem on the anonymity required of those who refused to toe the party line:

Creation calls for self-surrender,
Not loud noise and cheap success.
Life must be lived without false face,
Lived so that in the final count
We draw unto ourselves love from space.

So plunge yourself into obscurity
And conceal there your tracks.
But be alive, alive your full share,
Alive until the end.[20]

Pasternak wrote only one novel in his life, but he considered it his masterpiece and the summation of his life's work. *Doctor Zhivago* is an "inner history" of twentieth-century Russia that contrasts the private experiences of its finest citizens against the tumultuous changes in world history. The critic Nicola Chiaromonte describes the work as "a meditation on the infinite distance which separates the human conscience from the violence of history and permits a man to remain a man, to rediscover the track of truth that the whole whirlwind of events continually cancels and confuses."[21] The key to rediscovering the track of truth lies in the capacity of love to seek that which exists beyond itself and in the process transform all things into signs and symbols of the transcendent.

20. Boris Pasternak, "To Be Famous," in *Silver and Steel: 20th Century Russian Poetry: An Anthology,* ed. Yevgeny Yevtushenko (New York: Doubleday, 1994), 213, 214.
21. Nicola Chiaromonte, "The Paradox of History," in *Pasternak: Modern Judgments,* ed. Donald Davie and Angela Livingstone (London: Macmillan, 1969), 234.

The work is often misread, because it is a poet's novel, a symbolic work, not a realist fiction in the tradition of Turgenev or Tolstoy, and because it was published in the West during the Cold War after it had already been rejected by Soviet publishers. When Pasternak won the Nobel Prize in 1958, the Soviets saw the award as a propaganda attempt by the West to elevate a second-rate anti-Soviet novelist to the front ranks of world literature, and so forbade him from accepting the prize. Soviet critics blasted *Zhivago* as a species of failed socialist realism, misreading its form, undervaluing its lyricism, and totally ignoring its symbolic character; while many Western readers misappropriated the work as an anti-communist tract, oversimplifying its complex message, undervaluing its artistic integrity, and missing its ascetic spirituality. "What Pasternak opposes to Communism," the Trappist monk and spiritual writer Thomas Merton wrote, "is not a defense of Western Democracy, not an alternative political platform, not a formal religion, but *life itself* and leaves us to ponder the consequences."[22]

The novel (also terribly misrepresented by David Lean's movie, which captures all its images and none of its ideas) illustrates how easy it is to succumb to amorality in the name of historical necessity, and how easy it is for people to fall into playing parts in a social drama they misconceive, abandoning their integrity for the greater drama of an artificial existence. Yuri and Lara, like many other educated men and women of their generation, welcomed the Revolution and yet, despite its betrayal, continued to make sacrifices for Russia. They understood their place in history much differently than those who ruled them, and so their lives witnessed to a deeper, spiritual vision still living in internal exile within the Soviet system.

Honest Russians like Yuri and Lara welcomed the Second World War because it offered them the opportunity to do away with the lies of the People's Republic. But after the war, when things began to fall back into the same old distortions, a sense of inner resentment and betrayal began

22. Thomas Merton, *Disputed Questions* (New York: Harcourt Brace Jovanovich, 1985), 13.

to grow. In this sense, *Doctor Zhivago* is a great mandala of psychological and philosophical responses to the Russian Revolution and its aftermath—with Yuri and Lara at its moral/intellectual center—unconvinced by Soviet ideology—remaining true to the lost promise of Russian high modernist culture.

It was left to Solzhenitsyn, however, to turn this inner resolve into outward rebellion, and by so doing expose the limitations of Pasternak's literary "no" to power by adding his own brave "yes" to active noncooperation with evil. Pasternak's contribution to Russian history was to excise Russian Orthodoxy's unconscious collaboration with Marx, and though he may have gone too far in his advocacy of a necessary, almost monastic, isolation from the powers that be, his tragic Christian vision helped pave the way for Solzhenitsyn's dissident faith.

In *The Oak and the Calf,* Solzhenitsyn's literary memoir, he tells of his response to Pasternak being awarded the Nobel Prize in 1958. Solzhenitsyn was teaching physics in a high school on the outskirts of Siberia at the time, just a few years out of the camps, still burying his unpublishable novels in his backyard, furtively looking over his shoulder for the KGB.

He remarks how deeply envious he was of Pasternak's opportunity to live the destiny he had set for himself. Pasternak would go to Stockholm, never to return, but before exiled he would give the Nobel Prize speech to end all Nobel Prize speeches: boldly exposing the lies of the state, cutting the Soviet empire's moral authority off at the knees. Then he would publish all the works he had buried in *his* backyard—changing Russia, changing the world, and testifying to the power of the word over political tyranny and injustice.

But, of course, it didn't happen. Pasternak didn't accept his prize, didn't defy the authorities, and died a year later. It turned out there weren't any explosive secret manuscripts waiting to be published and that Pasternak was not a hardened gulag ex-con ready to take on the regime in a life-and-death struggle, but the tender last shoot of a decimated intellectual class, like Yuri Zhivago. Is it any wonder he died a year later of a broken heart?

Solzhenitsyn, however, was mortified by Pasternak's lack of radical energy. Now he himself had to win the Nobel Prize and do what Pasternak should have done. Solzhenitsyn writes:

> Never, not even in my young days, let alone as a hard-bitten zek [prisoner], have I been able to understand those who allow attachments to prevail over duty. (No one could have made me understand at the time that Pasternak had already published and said what he had to say, and that the missing Stockholm speech might have turned out to be no more awe-inspiring than his apologias in the newspapers.)
>
> All the more vividly did I see it, all the more eagerly did I brood on it, demand it from the future! I had to have that prize! As a position to be won, a vantage point on the battlefield! And the earlier I got it, the firmer I should stand, the harder I should hit! My behavior then would be the opposite in every way of Pasternak's. I should resolutely *accept* the prize, resolutely go to Stockholm, make a very resolute speech. Obviously, the road back would be closed to me. But I would be able to publish everything! Tell all I knew! Touch off the explosive charge that had been piling up since I first saw the box cells of the Lubyanka, through all those winter work parades in step lock; speak for all those who had been stifled, shot, starved or frozen to death! Drag it all to the platform of the Nobel Prize ceremony and hurl it like a thunderbolt. For all this, the lot of an outcast was not too high a price to pay.[23]

The foundation of Solzhenitsyn's aesthetics of resistance rests upon his plebeian mythopoetic conception of Christianity as the practice of virtue (as opposed to Marx's modernist conception of it as mystified ideology). Plebeians, like primitives, beatniks and nonviolent soldiers of truth, use transcendence as a way of making sense out of their own resistance to the world—not as a balm for present suffering or a means for indulging

---

23. Aleksandr Solzhenitsyn, *The Oak and the Calf,* trans. Harry Willetts (New York: Harper & Row, 1979), 292.

in the irrational. For plebeians, religious beliefs are survival techniques (necessities), and the incredible premise of a prime mover is their trump card against all the power brokers and social Darwinists of this world who would define them in terms of their own projects, ambitions, and ideological distortions. This is why Solzhenitsyn finds the inspiration for his resistance to the Soviet regime in the inmates (*zeks*) of the Gulag and not in the modernist masters in the West.[24]

The Western modernists did not always begin with the plebeian's incredible premise of a divine order behind the flux of experience. Most of them moved still further into the flux itself in order to further destabilize an already tottering status quo. For Solzhenitsyn, such a strategy played into the hands of the state philosophers and would-be tyrants and proved far too thin a countermeasure to deal meaningfully with the reality of the camps and the triumph of Marxist dialectics. The magnitude of the suffering demanded writing that could somehow break through both the intellectual impotence of the dying order and the reductionist terror of the ascending new methodologies. What was needed was a new expression of moral presence and transcendent hope—a new eschatological vision of the now. Someone had to testify to the reality of something outside dialectical redefinition and historical change in order to create a handle with which we could pull ourselves free from cultural relativism and the ascendant new nihilism.

In the camps, Solzhenitsyn discovered the absolute upon which to found this moral presence: the sanctity of individual conscience. But unlike in premodern times, integrity of person was no longer a birthright, and it could not be assumed that it was possessed by every mortal soul.

---

24. There is a wonderful little footnote in *The Oak and the Calf* where Solzhenitsyn tells of a request by Jean Paul Sartre to visit him. Solzhenitsyn had just become famous, and everyone wanted to meet the author of *A Day in the Life of Ivan Denisovich*. Solzhenitsyn declines the invitation. Western intellectuals, he tells us, especially political ideologues like Sartre, use their meetings with Eastern writers to further their own political agendae, while the moral authority of the suffering Russian writer is being exploited. Sartre would be able to cast the meeting any way he saw fit, without Solzhenitsyn having a way to respond. Solzhenitsyn remarks, "If only it had been someone other than Sartre! . . . I wonder whether he [Sartre] discerned in my refusal the depths of our aversion to him" (119). The only Western writer Solzhenitsyn disliked more was Bertrand Russell.

In Solzhenitsyn's postmodern world, integrity was something that had to be won back, earned, and recreated. The experience of the camps brought this shocking truth home to him. Just as Heidegger argued that the real problem of modernity is not that we have forgotten the question of Being but that we have forgotten that we have forgotten the question of Being, Solzhenitsyn comes to the equally startling conclusion that moderns have lost not only their moral center but their awareness that they have lost their moral center. In other words, amorality had been established through the triumph of dialectics as a form of higher consciousness, when in fact it represented the death of the intellectual conscience. In the West many critics assumed modernism to have triumphed over the positivisms of the early twentieth century. But literary modernism itself may have simply been another manifestation of the positivist desire to conquer life via theory.

Pasternak was Solzhenitsyn's precursor in this regard. He understood that history was not the story of the rise and fall of empires, but of intertwining destinies, and that the goal of life is not to conquer life but to purify one's heart. In a moving passage toward the end of the first volume of the *Gulag*, Solzhenitsyn tells of the time he was sitting on a bench between two KGB guards in a train depot. His transfers to new camps were the only times he was among free people. As he sat there, he reflected upon the petty concerns of people around him and how he longed to tell them the truth.

> And how do you bring it home to them? By an inspiration? By a vision? A dream? Brothers! People! Why has life been given you? In the deep, deaf stillness of midnight, the doors of the death cells are being swung open—and the great-souled people are being dragged out to be shot.[25]

But then Solzhenitsyn answers his own question. And to the reader's amazement, it is free from anger and resentment.

---

25. Aleksandr Solzhenitsyn, *The Gulag Archipelago: Volume One,* trans. Thomas P. Whitney (New York: Harper, 1975), 591.

If you want I'll spell it out for you right now. Do not pursue what is illusory—property and position: all that is gained at the expense of your nerves decade after decade, and is confiscated in one fell night. Live with a steady superiority over life—don't be afraid of misfortune and do not yearn for happiness; it is after all, all the same: the bitter never lasts forever, and the sweet never fills the cup to overflowing.[26]

Such a remark may appear stoic, but Solzhenitsyn goes beyond resignation to an absolute identification with his enemies that transforms his heroic resistance into compassion, wisdom, and the ultimate forgiveness. He continues:

Rub your eyes and purify your heart—and prize above all else in the world those who love you and wish you well. Do not hurt them or scold them, and never part with them in anger; after all you simply do not know: it might be the last act before your arrest. . . . But the convoy guards stroke the black handles of the pistols in their pockets. And we sit there, three in a row, sober fellows, quiet friends.[27]

Solzhenitsyn does not refute the system that imprisoned him; he utterly destroys its authority from within through an act of moral courage and spiritual witness. It is as a writer that Solzhenitsyn defeats the gulag. And although he is quick to point out that words are not enough to defeat injustice, his book and its worldwide impact make clear that authentic human expression can change the way the world sees itself and thereby change the world.

For Pasternak and Solzhenitsyn, words can still escape the relations of power and, in Foucault's phrase, acquire "an inverse energy—a discharge" against the prevailing "regime of truth." Such revolutionary speech is spoken one-to-one, between solitudes. Its source is individual souls—specific, breathing, working, loving, suffering people. And so, for Solzhenitsyn, the artist has an important role to play—not as the antenna of the race, but

26. Ibid.
27. Ibid., 592

as its moral ground. The task is not to forge in the smithy of one's soul the uncreated conscience of the race, but to resuscitate the conscience that never died.

Spiritual rebirth, however, was needed on both sides of the Iron Curtain, as Solzhenitsyn was to find out when he moved to America in the late 1970s. The Beat Generation writers, particularly Jack Kerouac, had addressed the problem of America's spiritual anomie two decades before, prefiguring a new role for American literature as the spiritual counterpoint to an increasingly cynical and self-satisfied consumer culture.

Jack Kerouac: "After Me, the Deluge"

By the late 1940s the Beats found themselves on the outside of the postwar economic bubble, looking not in but glancing ever farther outward. Disillusioned with the self-conscious decadence of their close friends from New York, they viewed not only the contemporary literary trends and philosophical fashions but also the sociopolitical climate as preventing intimate connection with the universal laws of the cosmos. In response, they constructed a theology of experience from cultural materials that were available to them.

John Lardas, *The Bop Apocalypse*[28]

The true work is our belief: true belief in immortal good; the continual human struggle against linguistic abstraction: recognition of the soul beneath everything, & humor. This is the return of the will.

Jack Kerouac, Sketch notebook #3[29]

Jack Kerouac once called himself a "strange solitary crazy Catholic mystic." Ginsberg called him that "American Lonely Prose Trumpeter of drunken Buddha Sacred Heart" who embarked on a spiritual quest "for

28. John Lardas, *The Bop Apocalypse* (Urbana: University of Illinois Press, 2001), 128.
29. Sketch notebook #3, entry 31 October 1952, quoted in Ben Giamo, *Kerouac: The Word and the Way* (Carbondale: Southern Illinois Press, 2000), 67.

the ultimate meaning of existence and suffering, and the celebration of joy in the meantime."[30] His life and his work were one long, sustained experiment in the art of conjoining spiritual living to literary form. He believed that literature was "a tale that's told for companionship and to teach something religious, of religious reverence, about real life, in this world."[31]

His style and worldview grew out of a neo-realist narrative aesthetic inspired by Joyce and evolved into a spontaneous bop prosody in which he tried to create a running verse narrative of the holy revelations constantly pouring through his mind. In *Doctor Sax: Faust Part Three*, Kerouac drew a portrait of a redeemed Faust, a magician whose ambitions served the innocent, whose magic was aimed at defeating the Serpent and who sought to bring about a restoration of Blakelike innocence, transforming the fall into grace. At the end of the novel, the Bird of Paradise does away with the Serpent, and we are left to contemplate a cosmos that is unimpressed by our "magic," a cosmos that can take care of itself. This, for Kerouac, is the postmodern religious revelation we must all come to eventually: God is not impressed by our Faustian magic!

In his quest to tell us everything that ever happened to him to bring him to this revelation, he moved from romantic lyricism to the ecstatic joy of pure being, back down to the void-pit of the Great World Snake, to the joyous pain of amorous love, and, finally, descended into a Catholic/ Buddhist serenity of penitential martyrdom. Through his writing, John Clellon Holmes remarked, "an open circuit of feeling was established between his awareness and its object of the moment, and the result was as startling as being trapped in another man's eyes."[32] But I would go even further and say the result is as startling as seeing through our own eyes *for the very first time*. Kerouac set out to do nothing less than to narrate

30. Allen Ginsberg, quoted in Ann Charters, *Kerouac: A Biography* (New York: St. Martin's Press, 1994), 9.

31. Jack Kerouac, *Satori in Paris* (New York: Grove Press, 1966), 10.

32. John Clellon Holmes, "The Great Remember," in Holmes, *Nothing More to Declare* (New York: Dutton, 1967 [1958]), quoted in *Jack Kerouac: On the Road—Text and Criticism*, ed. Scott Donaldson (New York: Penguin, 1979), 590.

"soul" perceptions to an increasingly soulless American middle class hungry for revelations of life's everyday holy radiance.

"Kerouac's talent as a writer," Ann Charters tells us, "was not his inventiveness with new characters and plots, but rather his power to dramatize the spirit of his own life into romantic fantasy."[33] This ability to mythologize his own experiences made him susceptible to the old antinomian heresy that as an artist he was exempt from orthodox morality. And yet, like Blake and Joyce before him, Kerouac never thought of himself as "morally exempt" from anything. His experience of sin and inadequacy was, if anything, more acute than the average person's, and if his behavior was often unconventional and even transparently amoral, he never thought of himself as beyond God's judgment or better than other people. He once confessed, "I can turn pain to bliss in Mind—and vice versa. Been doin it 30 years (30 years turning bliss to pain.)"[34] The literary life was not a license to sin; it was, rather, a responsibility to own up to the truth about oneself. If Kerouac seems self-indulgent to less experimental souls, this may be more of a symptom of his personal honesty than any antinomian heresy.

Perhaps this is also why Kerouac is often misread by conservative critics as a spoiled, ungrateful sentimentalist incapable of registering the world-historical role America was shouldering during the Cold War. They accuse him of elevating art to the status of an alternative reality rather than using it to illuminate reality. Roger Kimball, for example, charged him with having an "adolescent longing for liberation from conventional manners and intellectual standards," given over to polymorphous sexuality, narcissism, a destructive absorption in drugs, criminality, irrationalism, naive political radicalism, anti-Americanism, pseudospirituality, a spurious infatuation with Eastern religions, and the elevation of pop music to a sociospiritual weapon.

Kimball sums up his complaint:

33. Charters, *Kerouac: A Biography*, 66–67.
34. Jack Kerouac, *Some of the Dharma* (New York: Penguin, 1997), 277.

In a word, the establishment of the Beat church was significant as a chapter in the moral and cultural degradation of our society. Regarded as a literary phenomenon, however, what the Beats produced exists chiefly as a kind of artistic anti-matter. What the Beats have bequeathed to us is actively bad, a corrupting as well as a corrupt phenomenon. Two things have kept what the Beats wrote in circulation: the academic maw with its insatiable appetite for verbal fodder of any kind, and the unhealthy craving for instances of psychopathology that the Beats not only exemplified but also helped to foster in their work and in their lives.[35]

This common disparagement of the Beats is questionable as a broad characterization, but it is particularly misguided when applied to Kerouac, who later in his life publicly distanced himself from the hippies and countercultural activists who claimed him for their own. In fact, Kerouac always considered himself a dyed-in-the-wool American patriot and conservative Catholic whose three-year detour into Buddhism only deepened his faith in Christ. As early as 1954, in a letter to William Burroughs he said that the "Buddha is only for the West to study as history, that it is a subject for understanding, and Yoga can profitably be practiced to that end. But it is not for the West an Answer, not a Solution. We must learn by acting, experiencing, and living, that is, above all by Love and Suffering."[36]

What critics like Roger Kimball don't get about the Beats in general and Kerouac in particular is that it is just as possible to be unhappy in a wonderful environment as it is to be hopeful in a difficult one.[37] And that this capacity for unhappiness amid great material plenty is not necessarily a symptom of ingratitude toward America's socioeconomic gains, political liberties, or modern technological miracles. Human beings are not just organisms in environments or subjects within history, but individual

35. Roger Kimball, "A Gospel of Emancipation," *New Criterion* 15, no. 2 (October 1997): 8.

36. Jack Kerouac, *Selected Letters: 1940–1956,* ed. Ann Charters (New York: Penguin, 1996), 439.

37. I am reminded of a conversation I had with one of my students who spent a year working in an orphanage in one of the poorest countries in the world. He told me, "With all the training I got, I thought I was ready for anything. But I was surprised by the joy."

souls working out their own salvation amid great worldly suffering and injustice. We all, as Dostoyevsky and Kierkegaard well noted, possess transcendent longings that are inherently "romantic" (often even antinomian) and make culture, language, and symbolic expression an inherent "criticism of life," not just an illumination of reality.

Literature, even in the best of times, is never just the expression of universal truths or moral insight; it is also a tool for unlocking and disclosing the untapped spiritual possibilities inherent in one's time. Of course, it isn't just that either—hence, Kerouac's need to distance himself from his "Gnostic" peers and from the academic literary world bent on reducing his art to self-therapy.

In his essay "After Me, the Deluge" published in the *Los Angeles Times* in 1969, Kerouac criticizes the hippies and the beatniks and then asks the reader, "Ever look closely at anybody and see that particularized patience all their own, eyes hid, waiting with lips sewn down for time to pass, for something to succeed, for the long night of life to take them in its arms and say, 'Ah, Cherubim, this silly, stupid business. . . . What is it, existence?'"[38] Those who gravitate to Kerouac's outrage often miss this tender sympathy for those "inconsolable orphans."

"When James Joyce gave up 'sin,'" Kerouac reminds us, "he wanted to become the Virgin Mary's Knight."[39] And so if Kerouac finds beauty in jazz, deviants, prostitutes, drug addicts, hobos, and all the other unexpected places Christ is found, haven't we ourselves always suspected as much? It's just that we never took the time (or the risks) to explore those other worlds, and the fact that Kerouac *did*, that he dared to seek out beauty and dignity everywhere and describe its contours with loving attention, invites us to do the same.

When we read him, we take our own spiritual/aesthetic journeys into that great, vast unwashed American pandemic with equally loving eyes. "Since everything is surface ripples of manifestation, they neither abide

38. Jack Kerouac, *The Portable Jack Kerouac*, ed. Ann Charters (New York: Penguin, 1996), 578.

39. Kerouac, *Some of the Dharma*, 286.

in the past or in the future, but in some timeless present beyond the time of the body and the brain that dreams—So I have only ONE BOOK to write, in which everything, past, present, and future—everything that I know and everything that I did know and will know, and never knew and will never know, is caught like dust in the sunlight in the bedroom, immemorially shining in the mind essence sea which is its base and origin."[40]

Was he wrong to commit this literary indelicacy? Did his untamed enthusiasm end up glorifying ugliness and besmirching the good? Was his death by alcoholism final proof of his spiritual failure? In the end, I think, these are the wrong questions. The real question Kerouac's work poses to us is "to what extent can life be experienced as a revelation of holy sympathy in the very midst of suffering? How far can we open the door to loving kindness, compassion, gladness and equanimity? And at what point must we shut down, and defend ourselves against the pain love commands us to endure?" The ecstasy in Kerouac's prose is the ecstasy of Purgatory: to live it all again as regret.

"All I want to do is love," Kerouac wrote. "God will come into me like a golden light and make areas of washing gold above my eyes and penetrate my sleep with His Balm—Jesus, his Son, is in my Heart Constantly."[41]

Walker Percy: Beyond Existentialism

Kierkegaard recognized the unique character of the Christian gospel but, rather than see it as a piece of bona fide news delivered by a newsbearer, albeit news of divine origin . . . he felt obliged to set it over against knowledge as paradox. . . . Kierkegaard may have turned his dialectic against the Hegelian system, but he continued to appraise the gospel from the posture of the Hegelian scientist—and pronounced it absurd that a man's eternal

40. Kerouac, *Some of the Dharma*, 277.
41. Kerouac, quoted in Giamo, *The Word and the Way,* 87, from Kerouac's Sketch Notebook 1952–53.

happiness should depend not on knowledge sub species aeternitatis but on a piece of news from across the sea.

Walker Percy, *The Message in the Bottle*[42]

Although Walker Percy admired Kierkegaard, he transformed the Dane's existentialism through his articulation of a homemade philosophical anthropology. For Percy, like Kerouac, believed that Kierkegaard had got it only half right. To move out of the ethical realm into the religious did not demand a leap into the irrational so much as it did a long and thoughtful look around. We are already inside the mystery. Our selves and our absurdity are, in fact, the very same thing: a symptom of the knowing self's inability to grasp the larger context of its own experience within the great sea of love.

In his last book, *Lost in the Cosmos*, Percy tells us that if aliens from another planet ever landed on earth, our first question to them should be: "Did it happen to you too?" By this Percy means, did your calculative capacities come with an awareness of "self," or is your intelligence entirely the product of unconscious circuitry? Put another way, are you just very highly evolved ants, or do you have a soul? Are you human or machine?

Unlike ants, human beings act not as organisms living in an environment, but as "selves" operating in a "cosmos." Nature works dialectically through stimulus-response, and objects bumping into other objects; language, however, operates triadically through signs and objects mediated by "selves." To illustrate exactly what this means, Percy uses Helen Keller's account of her breakthrough into language, and hence into selfhood, dramatized in Arthur Penn's film of William Gibson's Pulitzer Prize-winning play, *The Miracle Worker*.

To recount the scene: Annie Sullivan is sitting at the family dinner table celebrating Helen's return to the family home after living in isolation

---

42. *The Message in the Bottle* (New York: Farrar, Straus & Giroux, 1975), 147, quoted in *Walker Percy and the Old Modern Age*, by Patricia Lewis Poteat (Baton Rouge: Louisiana State University Press, 1985), 132.

with Annie for two weeks of intense language training. Helen's father, a traditional Victorian patriarch, is ecstatic because Annie has succeeded in teaching the girl table manners. But Annie is frustrated because the child still hasn't grasped the fundamental symbolic connection between signs and things, between language and reality. She hasn't entered the triadic community and so is not yet a human being.

To see if the rigorous discipline established over the past two weeks still applies in her parents' home, Helen begins to forget her manners and drops her napkin. The mother wishes to let this indiscretion go uncorrected, but Annie demands that Helen pick it up. In defiance Helen sweeps her arm across the table, smashing the china, and sending her mother's roast flying across the room. She then takes a pitcher of water and splashes it in Annie's face.

Annie drags Helen outside and makes her refill the pitcher at the water pump. As she does so, she begins for the millionth time to sign words into Helen's hand and then place Helen's hands upon the signed objects.

"Pump!" Annie shouts, and thrusting Helen's hands to the pump handle, she signs "P-U-M-P."

"Water!" she shouts, and thrusts Helen's hands under the streaming, cold water as she signs "W-A-T-E-R."

It is clear that Annie is not doing this because she thinks Helen will learn this time but simply because she doesn't know what else to do. Helen continues to resist—crying, kicking, pushing, and pulling away.

Then, as instantly as it began, Helen's tantrum stops. She becomes quiet, absorbed, perfectly still. Rapt with attention, she finally makes the connection between words and things, signs and experience, and for the first time in her life she grasps the idea that things have names! Helen whispers "Wa, Wa" and in that moment she is transformed from an organism in an environment to a self in the world, from an animal into a human being.

But then what happens next is every bit as moving and just as important.

She whirls around the yard trying to touch everything, thirsty for the signs to describe her world, the signs that give things their human reality.

"What's this?" Helen indicates, touching a post, "And this? And this? And this?"

Annie calls out to Helen's parents: "Mr. and Mrs. Keller! Come! Come! Helen knows. She *knows!*"

What does she know? She knows that humans share truth through signs, that she is not alone in her interior life, that there is a shape to human experience and that her every experience has a matching word and, hence, *a meaning*. This knowledge is, in essence, the awareness of what it means to be a human being. It is one's initiation into the human cosmos.

Helen's parents emerge from the dinning room, and Helen touches their faces and signs their names—knowing them as part of her human world for the very first time.

Then she stops and touches Annie's face.

Annie signs out the word "T-E-A-C-H-E-R," and she knows who it is that finally bridged her spiritual isolation.

This is what one might call a messianic moment, for from that moment on Annie and Helen share an intimacy far deeper than mere sentiment or shared existential longing. Annie is no longer just another obstacle in Helen's self-encased world, nor is she a parent limited by pity. She is something completely different, a doorway to the meaning of the universe. She is a *teacher;* what William Gibson calls "a miracle worker."

For Percy, Helen Keller's transformation from a sign-making animal to a reflective human being is a key parable for who we are; we are not existentially present absences so much as we are "selves" on the borderland between two worlds; between the dyadic animal world of stimulus-response and the triadic human world of mediated experience. What Helen experienced when she made the connection between the sign and the thing was not *the sign* or *the thing* but the third reality that connected them, "the self." In that moment, the water disappeared from her hands, and she grasped an inner picture of a shared, knowable, and communicable world. And so she turned back to everything she had ever experienced to find out its name.

The practical significance of this revelation of man as half animal—intoxicated by the experiences before him and abstracted from them at the same time—is explored in all of Percy's novels as his "heroes" move in and out of all kinds of relationships. In *Lost in the Cosmos* Percy asks,

> Why do people often feel bad in good environments and good in bad environments? Why did Mother Teresa think that affluent Westerners often seemed poorer than the Calcutta poor, the poorest of the poor?
>
> The paradox comes to pass because the impoverishments and enrichments of a self in a world are not necessarily the same as the impoverishments and enrichments of an organism in an environment. The organism is needy or not needy accordingly as needs are satisfied or not satisfied by its environment. The self in a world is rich or poor accordingly as it succeeds in identifying its otherwise unspeakable self, e.g., mythically, by identifying itself with a world-sign, such as a totem; religiously, by identifying itself as a creature of God. But totems don't work in a scientific age because no one believes, no matter how hard he tries, that he can "become" a tiger or a parakeet (cf. the depression of a Princeton tiger or Yale bulldog, one hour after the game).[43]

"The self" can be transcendent and "happy," while "the organism" is immanent and "anxious." The reverse is also true. No wonder we can't understand why it feels so bad in the best of all possible environments—"say, a good family and a good home in a good neighborhood in East Orange on a fine Wednesday afternoon." Or why we "secretly relish bad news, assassinations, plane crashes, and the misfortunes of neighbors"[44]—anything to escape the tedium of immanence. Percy explains:

> Enrichment in such an age appears either as enrichment within immanence, i.e., the discriminating consumption of the goods and services of society, such as courses in personality enrichment, creative play, and self-growth through

43. Walker Percy, *Lost in the Cosmos* (New York: Picador, 1983), 121–23.
44. Ibid., 122.

group interaction, etc.—or through the prime joys of the age, self-transcendence through science and art. The pleasure of such transcendence derives not from the recovery of self but from the loss of self. Scientific and artistic transcendence is a partial recovery of Eden, the semiotic Eden, when the self explored the world through signs before falling into self-consciousness.[45]

Modern anthropology deals with man as a physical organism and with the products of man as a culture member, but not with man as a free-floating subject burdened by consciousness.[46]

If we cannot name a thing, we cannot know it except as it relates to our instinctual nature or physical existence.[47] Naming is the act that bridges the gap between the "behaviorism of Mead and the existentialism of Marcell"[48] by bringing objects into our personal cosmos of meaning, transforming them from things "out there" into meaningful objects "in-here." In other words, our identity as symbol makers provides an answer to the mind-body problem in a way that physicalism and dualism cannot. It dissolves the distinction between words and things into the activity of naming. To be is to name. I name, therefore I coexist.

For Percy, our use of symbols is not a dyadic stimulus-response event, as most semioticians and language theorists view it. Symbol-mongering cannot be explained by behaviorist theory or as a succession of energy states. This realization, for Percy, shatters

the old dream of the Enlightenment—that an objective-explanatory-causal science can discover and set forth all the knowledge of which man is capable. . . . Man is not merely a higher [purely biological] organism responding to and controlling his environment. He is, in Heidegger's words, that being in the world whose calling it is to find a name for Being, to give testimony to it, and to provide for it a clearing.[49]

45. Ibid., 122–23.
46. Percy, *Message in the Bottle*, 239.
47. Walker Percy, *Signposts in a Strange Land* (New York: Picador, 1991), 261, 274, 282.
48. Percy, *Message in the Bottle*, 272.
49. Ibid., 158.

Why do current anthropological and semiotic theories fail to adequately describe the nature of man? Simply because, while they can adequately account for cause-effect actions, responses to stimuli, survival and instinctual behavior, they do not explain what a symbol is, because a symbol is not part of a dyadic event; it exists only as part of a three-way relationship in which experience is given a name and therefore shared and intensified. In other words, symbols are not things and not feelings, but something else.

When human beings use words and phrases, they are not responding to stimuli; they are *symbolizing:* sharing worlds. Somehow we all get the joke that the name is and isn't the thing at the same time. It *is* the thing in the collective mind's agreement to call the thing that name—but it *isn't literally the thing* itself. It is the thing only as it exists in the imaginary, humanly shared cosmos created by the naming.

This "revelation" of the simultaneous presence and absence of language opens the floodgates to a world of meanings that cohere but do not actually mirror the real world, thus giving birth to duality, metaphysics, art, culture, civilization, and consciousness itself. Individuals enter this "cosmos" through the door of revelation made possible by triadic events that are not reducible to dyadic cause and effect. Language is a non-linear, non-energetic natural phenomenon.

Percy calls this event "the Delta Factor" (referring to the delta-shaped triangle created when you diagram this phenomenon).[50]

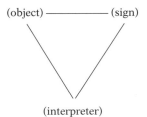

(object) ——————— (sign)

(interpreter)

50. Ibid., 39.

To give something a name, he tells us, is at "first sight the most commonplace of events, but in reality, a most mysterious act."[51] "A sign-using
organism takes account only of those elements of its environment which
are relevant biologically . . . but a symbol-using organism has a world."[52]
A world entails "naming" and lamentations for events, for what happened
yesterday, for what happened "in the beginning," and has no "gaps." A
world has myths. "Chickens have no myths," Percy explains.[53]

> The greatest difference between the environments (Umwelt) of the sign-
> using organism and the world (Welt) of the speaking organism is that there
> are gaps in the former but none in the latter. The non-speaking organism
> only notices what is relevant biologically; the speaking organism disposes
> of the entire horizon symbolically. Gaps that cannot be closed by percep-
> tion and reason are closed by magic and myth.[54]

For Percy, the inability to name is the real cause of human anxiety.
This anxiety can range from "slight uneasiness to terror in the face of the
uncanny."[55] The act of communication provides existential healing, for
it enables the speaker's imaginary "self" to connect with both material
reality and the human community. In other words, though the word is
not really one with the object, though it makes a play at approximat-
ing the object, the word enables a grasping and an understanding of
the object as part of a universe of meanings (or cosmos).[56] Hence the
transformational spiritual joy Helen Keller experienced when she first
understood the word *water.*

This dynamic is central for Percy because contemporary society is
losing touch with its communal and unifying myths. The "self" is rich
only to the degree it succeeds in identifying its place and purpose in a

51. Ibid., 254.
52. Ibid., 202.
53. Ibid.
54. Ibid., 203.
55. Ibid., 136.
56. J. P. Telotte, "A Symbolic Structure for Walker Percy's Fiction," in *Critical Essays on Walker Percy,* ed. Donald Crowley and Sue Mitchell Crowley (Boston: G. K. Hall, 1989), 172.

world.[57] For thousands of years, myth enabled us to find ourselves in a world, to know who we were, and what our lives meant. The twentieth century, with its metaphysical skepticism and reductionist science, severed that connection, so now mankind, according to Percy, is "lost in the cosmos."

The problem with modern psychiatry and current philosophical attempts to understand mankind is that they treat humanity as a biological organism with instinctive drives and needs, and little beyond that. These disciplines, Percy tells us, don't offer any "account of man as possessing a unique destiny by which he is oriented in a wholly different direction," and as a result "these fields have almost nothing to say about the great themes that have engaged the existential critics of modern society from Søren Kierkegaard to Gabriel Marcel."[58] As Percy put it in his National Book Award acceptance speech, "man is more than an organism in an environment, more than an integrated personality, more even than a mature and creative individual, as the phrase goes. He is a wayfarer and a pilgrim."[59] In other words, a seeker of meanings, a metaphysical bridge builder, a "self."

In Percy's novels he narrates the endless paradoxes and contradictions the experience of "selfhood" foists upon us—exploring the dynamics of the inner life in a postexistential world where private meanings and public events are everywhere in collision. In his first novel, *The Moviegoer*, Percy's hero Binx Bolling sought to live with the same kind of intensity and significance that he found only in the movies. Binx remarks, "To become aware of the possibility of the search is to be onto something. Not to be onto something is to be in despair."[60] He feels that he is living among dead people, "automatons who have no choice in what they say," and seeks to find, for himself, some way of transforming the mundane into the significant.[61] Although the novel ends on a note of hope, it really isn't until Percy's later works, such as *The Second*

---

57. Percy, *Lost in the Cosmos*, 122.
58. Percy, *Signposts*, 252.
59. Ibid., 246.
60. Walker Percy, *The Moviegoer* (New York: Vintage, 1998 [1961]), 13.
61. Ibid., 100.

Coming and *Love in the Ruins,* that Percy discovers "the Delta Factor" and makes it clear that revelation lies waiting all around us.

These later novels dramatize the quest for meaning of the postmodern "self" and mirror the ache of our incessant longings for spiritual completeness in a world where this need can never be fully answered. This irresoluable tension is especially acute in the realm of politics, where the fathomless depths of the self run headlong into the problems of "organisms in environments" involving those who are "onto something" in a slough of contradictions where they must struggle to reconcile the exigencies of the moment with the dreams of visionary possibility.

3

Antipolitical Politics

We live in a time when it is harder for a free man to make a home than it was for a medieval ascetic to do without one.

G. K. Chesterton, *Outline of Sanity*[1]

What is the expression which the age demands? The age demands no expression whatever. We have seen photographs of bereaved Asian mothers. We are not interested in the agony of your fumbled organs. There is nothing you can show on your face that can match the horror of this time. Do not even try. You will only hold yourself up to the scorn of those who have felt things deeply. We have seen newsreels of humans in the extremes of pain and dislocation. Everyone knows you are eating well and even being paid to stand up there. You are playing to people who have experienced a catastrophe. This should make you very quiet. Speak the words, convey the data, and step aside. Everyone knows you are in pain. You cannot tell the audience

1. G. K. Chesteron, *Outline of Sanity* (London: Methuen, 1928), 119.

everything you know about love in every line of love you speak.
Step aside and they will know what you know because they know
it already. You have nothing to teach them. You are not more
beautiful than they are. You are not wiser. Do not shout at them.

Leonard Cohen, "How to Speak Poetry"[2]

Modern novelists may have diagnosed our current spiritual situation with clarity and power, but their visions must be transformed into practice if we really want to test their value as criticisms of life. The Christian social activists examined in this section bring visionary standards to bear on the social realities of their times. Each of them advocate what Václav Havel calls "antipolitical politics," politics *not as an art of manipulation or rule over others* but as a way of achieving meaningful lives together, politics as "practical morality, as service to the truth, as essentially human and humanly measured care for our fellow humans."[3] Their collective work constitutes the beginning of a unified front against the "political politics" of both left- and right-wing ideologues, carrying forward Chesterton's notions of decentralization and "distributism" into the twenty-first century. At first glance, this road not taken may seem a bit anachronistic and nostalgic, but for those for whom the Beatitudes still remain the last word in social ethics, it deserves a hard and close second look.

According to these religious theorist-practitioners, the primary threat to human autonomy no longer comes from "nature" or from "tyrants" but from economic, political, and social systems of our own making that have become increasingly powerful, increasingly self-perpetuating, and increasingly out of control. The men and women who operate these systems benefit by them and defend them with their lives but don't really understand the impact they have on other individuals or cultures. And

2. Leonard Cohen, *Stranger Music* (New York: Vintage, 1993), 287–88.
3. Václav Havel, "Politics and Conscience," quoted in Jan Vladislav, ed., *Václav Havel: Living in Truth* (London: Faber, 1989), 155.

even if they did, they wouldn't be able to do much about it given the complexities of the systems they serve and the enormity of the problems they face.

As a result, our leaders rely upon experts to tell them which levers of the government machinery to pull and which gears of the economic engine to engage, without they themselves truly understanding the full effects of their actions. And so these leaders end up perpetuating—despite whatever good intentions they might possess—the very injustices, inequalities, and miseries they claim to be trying to eliminate.

Americans, in particular, have been the victims of a myth of national "exceptionalism," which has been used over and over again to promote policies that have the immediate impact of separating individuals from their land and capital. Between 1983 and 1998, the net worth of the top 1 percent grew by 42.2 percent, while the net worth of the bottom 40 percent dropped by 76.3 percent. In other words, the bottom 40 percent of the United States population lost three-fourths of their family wealth over the past twenty years.[4]

As of 1998, the top 1 percent of Americans owned 95 percent of the country's assets, and the top 60 percent own 99.8 percent of the nation's wealth.[5] Despite the claim that a 401(k) plan constitutes corporate ownership for the masses, owning mutual funds actually puts the average person more at the mercy of the companies they own than when they lived off the land or hid their savings under a mattress.

On a global scale the shift of capital into fewer and fewer hands has been even more pronounced. According to the 1999 United Nations

4. These figures are taken from Edward N. Wolff, "Recent Trends in Wealth Ownership," a paper for the conference on "Benefits and Mechanisms for Spreading Asset Ownership in the United States," New York University, December 10–12, 1998. Edward N. Wolff's principal research areas are productivity growth and the distribution of income and wealth, and he is currently engaged in a project called "The Long-Term Effects of Technological Change and Information Technology on Earnings, Inequality, and Labor Demand." The project explores some of the long-run implications of technological change and information technology on the structure of labor demand and earnings. He is a professor of economics at New York University and author of many books, including *Top Heavy: A Study of the Increasing Inequality of Wealth in America* (New York: New Press, 2002).

5. Ibid.

Development Report, eighty countries have per capita incomes lower than they were a decade ago, and the assets of the world's two hundred richest people total more than the combined assets of 41 percent of the world's population—that's more than the combined wealth of two billion people.[6]

As a result, local concerns have become increasingly regionalized, regional concerns increasingly nationalized, and national concerns increasingly internationalized. This has had the overall effect not of making people more globally responsible but of making them more xenophobic and wary, perpetually scanning the horizon for incoming threats and approaching global disasters.

The alternative proposed by Christian social critics to this growing occupation by the forces of international capital is for ordinary citizens to take back responsibility for their own material well-being through *more capitalism*, not less; that is to say, through *a greater distribution of capital* as opposed to its greater centralization. By building upon Dorothy Day's example of self-sustaining farms, family businesses, economically autonomous communities and households, more and more individuals could become secure from the would-be Caesars of this world, thus making possible a true alternative to the top-down hierarchical organization of the human enterprise.

To accomplish this radical reordering of priorities, however, policies must be encouraged that will *increase the economic autonomy* of families and small communities. Capital must be redirected toward local, environmentally sustainable projects and collectives. Our national security can best be sustained through decentralization, smaller power grids, and greater commercial diversity. This is even more true in an age of terrorism. The Christian solution, insofar as it is exemplified by the thinker-activists examined here, advocates smaller corporate units and greater

6. This report, as well as more recent ones, is available online from the United Nations at www.undp.org/hdro/.

economic diversity, flexibility, and security: not a new crusade in defense of Empire.

Perhaps one of the reasons Dorothy Day's writings have had more staying power than those of her communist comrades from the thirties—or her capitalist critics from the fifties and sixties—is that her Christian personalism clued her into the false promises of both the left and the right, and so her reforms were never the expression of sentimental revolutionary logic or free market ideology, but the product of hard-won, concrete insights born of real service to the poor. She knew what Walker Percy understood so well, that human beings are not just organisms in environments but selves in a cosmos.

Likewise, Martin Luther King Jr.'s greatest contributions to our time were his grassroots movements for the redress of specific social injustices in the name of the people actually enduring them, not his support of any abstract movement or cause. In fact, his measured commitment to Christian "personalism" and to "the beloved community" actually cost him political influence to the more ideologically extreme—and easier to fathom—Black Power revolutionaries. And yet he held the line, opting for a more difficult, even "unsuccessful" witness for nonviolence over his enemies' immediate, but ultimately pyrrhic, victories.

E. F. Schumacher and Wendell Berry, heirs to G. K. Chesterton and Dorothy Day, also recommend a return to the values of small, autonomous neighborhoods and family enterprises as a way of empowering the Christian "self" with its longings for metaphysical completion and social justice. In fact, Schumacher's slogan "Think Globally, Act Locally" has helped reshape the insurgent political thinking of our time away from an Althusserian search for a "theory of liberation" back to the workable attempt of reforming existing institutions and governments one by one.

Dorothy Day: On the Mysteries of Poverty and Activism

St. Augustine in his *City of God* says that God never intended man to dominate his fellows. He was to dominate the beasts of the field, the fowls of the air, what crawled upon the earth, but men were not to dominate each other. He preferred shepherds to kings. It was man himself who insisted on having a worldly king though he was warned what would happen to him. God allowed the prophets to anoint the kings and once men had accepted their kings they were supposed to show them respect, to obey the authority they had set up. To obey, that is, in all that did not go against their conscience. St. Peter was ordered by lawful authority not to preach in the name of Jesus, and he said he had to obey God rather than man, and he left prison to go out again to the market place and preach the Gospel. Over and over again, men had to disobey lawful authority to follow the voice of their conscience. This obedience to God and disobedience to the State has over and over again happened through history. It is time again to cry out against our "leaders," to question whether or not, since it is not for us to say that they are evil men, they are sane men.

Dorothy Day, "Are the Leaders Insane?"[7]

Dorothy Day went a long way toward solving the problem of social alienation through her activist demystification of the welfare state, laissez-faire capitalism, and the military-industrial complex. Her meditations on the mysteries of poverty and nonviolence began to heal the split between Christian acquiescence and social reform in creative new ways. For her, the key to solving seemingly insolvable social problems was simply to ask different questions. To change your life, change the way you process experience. And to change the way you process experience, change the way you live. We don't think our way into a new life; we live our way to new thoughts. The fact that she stopped short of articulating a full-blown socioeconomic theology makes her even more relevant to our time than more systematic theologians and social theorists, for she intuited

7. Dorothy Day, "Are the Leaders Insane?" *Catholic Worker* (April 1954): 1, 6. See also Dorothy Day Library on the Web at http://www.catholicworker.org/dorothyday/.

the dangers inherent in any sweeping ideological critique of economic injustice. She was not a philosopher but a Christian disciple, living the mythos, and learning her politics firsthand through her uncompromised attempt to live a Christian life.

Perhaps the hardest thing for people to grasp about Dorothy Day is that she was *not* a political ideologue. She would have loved Jacques Ellul's remark that "what constantly marked the life of Jesus was not nonviolence but in every situation the choice not to use power. This is infinitely different."[8] Attempts to systematize her thought inevitably fall short of doing justice to her witness, for she was not advocating any kind of synthesis of politics with religion so much as exploring their seeming incompatibility and subjecting the outbreak of global violence to a rigorous moral critique based upon her firsthand experiences living with the victims of history and the outcasts of society.

Her "pacifism" was more of an attempt to "desacralize" war. The militarization of the world and the production of weapons of mass destruction were setting the stage for even more horrendous human conflicts down the line: all in the name of universal justice, law, and order. Someone, somewhere had to say "no," had to fight historical "necessity" with the foolishness of Christ—even if the powers that be scoffed, the church flinched, and the world went on its merry way into the nuclear age.

She wrote:

> When it is said that we disturb people too much by the words pacifism and anarchism, I can only think that people need to be disturbed, that their consciences need to be aroused, that they do indeed need to look into their work, and study new techniques of love and poverty and suffering for each other. Of course the remedies are drastic, but then too the evil is a terrible one and we are all involved, we are all guilty, and most certainly we are all going to suffer. The fact that we have "the faith," that we go to

8. Jacques Ellul, *What I Believe*, trans. Geoffrey W. Bromiley (Grand Rapids: Eerdmans, 1989), 149.

the sacraments, is not enough. "Inasmuch as ye have done it unto the least of these my brethren, ye have done it unto me" with napalm, nerve gas, our hydrogen bomb, our "new look."[9]

The tartness of this remark reveals that Day was avant-garde in her rhetoric and style, innovative in her analyses of the sources of poverty and suffering amid progress, but orthodox in her commitment to the Catholic church and in her defense of the Beatitudes. Like G. K. Chesterton and Hilaire Belloc, she embraced "distributism" as an economic alternative to the new industrial ethics of both the communists and the capitalists. And like Berdyaev, she developed an existential critique of the new bourgeoisie that exposed the idol of progress worshiped by the new middle class and the revolutionary cadres.

The essence of distributism, as Chesterton spelled in out in his books *What Is Wrong with the World* and *The Outline of Sanity*, was the notion that everyone *should* own private property, that it should not be concentrated in the hands of the few, and that family farms, businesses, and property hold the best check against social and economic injustices and dehumanizing totalitarian schemes. The problem with capitalism was not "private property," but its accumulation in the hands of the few—its unfair *distribution*.

Dorothy Day was a repentant "anarchist" who had somehow found God, but a Catholic "distributist" who was working out her views of man and society in the streets and on the farms, through direct action. She never stopped thinking, writing, revising her views, and refining her ideas. She wanted workers to own their own businesses, thereby abolishing the assembly line. She also wanted to decentralize factories to restore work as craft. In other words, she envisioned monastery-like communities of like-minded families and friends: living together, off the land, producing goods and services that helped to build the City of God within the City of Man.

9. Ibid.

It isn't because resources are scarce that we require large-scale econo-mies and factories; it is because our wants are unlimited. And our wants are unlimited because our modern desires are not reflections of real needs so much as they are attempts to gain privilege and status by acquiring what we think other people want to possess. Economic ills are not entirely problems of material development; many of them simply reflect a lack of spiritual serenity and self-acceptance. The poor of this world are suffering—not only from a lack of land and capital but also from a failure to grasp what it is that would actually make them happy and thereby independent from the powers that be. This is the reason why the Gospels are "good news" to the poor: they reveal the essential emptiness of worldly prestige and replace it with the true joy of the beloved community.

Day remarked, "Under capitalism the many had not the opportunity of obtaining land and capital in any useful amount and were compelled by physical necessity to labor for the fortunate few who possessed these things. But the theory was all right. Distributists want to save the theory by bringing the practice in conformity with it."[10] Widespread ownership of property is the only check democracies have against the centralized state and monopoly capitalism, the only social force powerful enough to support local government, preserve local traditions, and keep communi-ties self-sufficient. Large-scale industrial economies work against human happiness by making everyone economically dependent on people and forces they don't know and forces they can't control. And in our era of global markets, this situation is becoming even worse.

In order to live with themselves, the rich—whose lives are built upon the industrial production of workers they never meet—require tokens of their personal entitlement, and this is accomplished through conspicu-ous consumption of rolling lawns, swimming pools, maids, gardens, and expensive sports cars. "Every *man-of-the-world*," Leon Bloy points out, "—whether he knows it or not—bears in himself an absolute contempt

---

10. Dorothy Day, *Catholic Worker*, June 1948. See also Dorothy Day Library on the Web at http://www.catholicworker.org/dorothyday/.

for poverty, and such is the deep secret honor which is the cornerstone of oligarchies."[11] Worldliness, in other words, is essentially the capacity to look past the unfair distribution of the world's wealth in order to affirm one's right to its spoils.

This is why the lives of the wealthy so often narrow into a game of waxing and waning delusions of grandeur in which they identify the fate of their financial interests with the fate of civilization itself. And since they cannot imagine living in equality with those who must sell their labor in the job market they themselves have transcended, the rich tend to favor "no laws at all." The political philosophy of the wealthy is libertarianism, drifting more and more toward anarchy as their capital increases.

But it isn't *being* rich that corrupts people; it's that in a world of unequal distribution, riches distance them from those who suffer. Not that *being* poor necessarily makes one ethically superior, but it can free one from a false identification with the privileges of bourgeois civilization. In practical terms, this means that Catholic Workers and Protestant missionaries, by living with the poor rather than with the rich, and by working to defend small businesses against larger ones and defending family farms against centralized agribusiness, do more than just keep alive a social vision of justice; they also purge themselves of materialist illusions and so keep themselves closer to the providence of God.

"If I have accomplished anything in my life," Day remarked, "it is because I wasn't embarrassed to talk about God." By writing about her social work in theological terms with honesty and integrity, she ended up narrating the tragicomic epic of her own personal spiritual journey—articulating its terrors and its solace, its victories and defeats, paradoxes and ironies, free from jargon, ideology, or cant.

She reminded us again and again that the first plank in the Catholic Worker Program was "clarification of thought," and so there could be no revolution without a theory of revolution. But by *theory*, she didn't mean ideology; she meant a willingness to consider the historical whole

11. Leon Bloy, *Pilgrim of the Absolute,* ed. Raissa Maritain, trans. John Coleman and Harry Lorin Binsse (London: Eyre and Spottiswoode, 1947), 165.

within which one lived, worked, and struggled. There is, she reminded us, such a thing as the heresy of good works—those "accursed occupations" that keep us from thinking. "To feed the hungry, clothe the naked and shelter the harborless without also trying to change the social order so that people can feed, clothe and shelter themselves, is just to apply palliatives. It is to show a lack of faith in one's fellows, their responsibilities as children of God, heirs of heaven."[12]

In the sixties, Catholic Workers protested the Vietnam War and became advisers for the growing antiwar movement—having counseled conscientious objectors during the Korean War and the Second World War. They were also a major part of the farm labor protests in California, and Day marched with Cesar Chavez and the United Farm Workers many times. This led to the Catholic Workers becoming identified with the counterculture, but as with Kerouac, this is somewhat of a misreading of their role and influence.

For Dorothy Day, social injustice demanded dissent, and—given the challenges and the political fault lines of her time—political protest simply came with the Christian territory. Her willingness to protest in the street has, for better and for worse, inspired anti-abortionists as well as nuclear protestors. But neither of these movements take seriously her admonishments to build alternative communities and to go back to the land to fight the social alienation brought about by both communism and industrial capitalism.

As with Chesterton before her and Thomas Merton after her, Day's ideas were never refuted, just misrepresented, overplayed, and then left for dead *in medias res*, another half-built cathedral, surviving on a thread of memory and the steel of committed disciples and friends. Rereading her today, one does not find a simple program for social reform so much as an existential critique of easy conscience. Dorothy Day didn't have all the answers, but she had all the right questions. Better than any we are asking today. But such a nontriumphalist vision is hard for us to appreciate these

12. Dorothy Day, "More About Holy Poverty," *Catholic Worker*, February 1945, 1–2.

days, given media that bleach the thought of even our most enlightened souls in the dye of misrepresentation, slander, and spin.

"Ask Me about My Vow of Silence": Thomas Merton's Social Activism of the Heart

> Real genius is nothing but the supernatural virtue of humility in the domain of thought.
>
> Simone Weil, "Human Personality"[13]

Thomas Merton was an orthodox Catholic his entire adult life, but avant-garde as a literary stylist and social thinker. He lived in a monastery, and later in a hermitage, but through extensive correspondence he also engaged in a variety of conversations with a multitude of contemporary thinkers from many different backgrounds and traditions, from Marxists to Sufis, from Protestants to Russian Orthodox, even from atheists to Zen masters.

As an aspiring poet, he identified with the Beats and the experimental writers of his era, founded an avant-garde literary journal, *Monk's Pond*, publicly opposed the Vietnam War, and just before his untimely death by accidental electrocution in 1968, gave a speech at an international meeting of monastics in Thailand. And although he was exploring the similarities between Western and Eastern contemplative traditions when he died, I suspect, given the topic of his last speech—"Marxism and Monastic Perspectives"—he was more likely on his way to becoming a liberation theologian than a Buddhist.

Merton's transcultural and ecumenical concerns were not based upon any Enlightenment theories of universal culture or Marxist notions of religion as "superstructure," but, like Dorothy Day's, upon a deep conviction that in our heart of hearts all of us are already one and that it is

---

13. Simone Weil, "Human Personality," in *The Simone Weil Reader*, ed. George A. Panichas (New York: McKay, 1977), 329.

our "false selves" or "surface identities" that continue to propagate the myths of inferiority, superiority, racism, nationalism, and ontological "difference." This is why Merton never thought of his decision to take holy orders as a retreat from the world so much as a refusal to participate in lies or support false actions. He wrote:

> As far as I can see, what I abandoned when I "left the world" and came to the monastery was the understanding of myself that I had developed in the context of civil society—my identification with what appeared to me to be its aims. Certainly, in the concrete, "the world" did not mean for me either riches (I was poor) or a life of luxury, certainly not the ambition to get somewhere in business or in anything else except writing. But it did mean a certain set of servitudes that I could no longer accept—servitudes to certain standards of value which to me were idiotic and repugnant and still are. Many of these were trivial, some of them were onerous, all are closely related. The image of a society that is happy because it drinks Coca-Cola or Seagrams or both and is protected by the bomb. The society that is imaged in the mass media and in advertising, in the movies, in TV, in best sellers, in current fads, in all the pompous and trifling masks with which it hides callousness, sensuality, hypocrisy, cruelty, and fear.[14]

After ten years of living under vows of silence, obedience, and chastity, Merton published his autobiography, which told the story of his conversion from a modern skeptic to a monastic contemplative. His ten years living outside the modern world, coupled with his scholastic training and the existential sensibility acquired as a young man coming of age in the tumultuous thirties, made his book one of the most eloquent and original defenses of individual spiritual responsibility of the entire postwar era. *The Seven Storey Mountain* quickly became an international best seller—catapulting him into instant celebrity and adding new depth and rigor to the postwar religious "boom."

14. Merton, *Conjectures of a Guilty By-Stander*, 36, 37.

In the 1950s his talks, to the postulants at the monastery at Gethse-
mane in Kentucky, were published in a series of book-length works that
signaled his transition away from the Manichean Catholicism expressed
in *The Seven Storey Mountain* to a new, more ecumenical understanding
of the faith. *New Seeds of Contemplation* and *No Man Is an Island* became
devotional classics.

In the sixties he applied his contemplative perspective to contemporary
social and political problems in such works as *Confessions of a Guilty
By-Stander* and *Seeds of Destruction,* which brought social criticism out
of its ideological cold war dichotomies by shifting terms away from the
rhetorical battle between progressives and conservatives into the quest
for a single unified expression of what it might mean to live life in accord
with conscience.

Over the next twenty years, Merton deepened his critique of the modern world in a series of increasingly discerning commentaries on contemporary life. He repudiated the sharp moral distinctions of his earlier
works, bringing the spiritual wisdom of Christianity, Buddhism, and
Sufism to bear on such issues as the arms race, civil rights, and the Vietnam War. "It seems to me," Merton wrote, "that the most basic problem
is not political, it is a-political and human. One of the most important
things to do is to keep cutting deliberately through political lines and
barriers and emphasizing the fact that these are largely fabrications and
that there is another dimension, a genuine reality, totally opposed to the
fictions of politics, the human dimension which politicians pretend to
abrogate entirely to themselves. Is this possible?"[15]

Merton spent the remainder of his life exploring this possibility. He
died by accidental electrocution while attending an international conference on monasticism in Bangkok, Thailand, in 1968—the very same year
Martin Luther King Jr. and Robert F. Kennedy were assassinated. This
put an end to one of the most spiritually charged decades in American

15. Thomas Merton, *The Hidden Ground of Love,* ed. William H. Shannon (New York: Harcourt
Brace Jovanovich, 1985), 272.

history, and yet, even after his death, Merton's work continued to be published, as scholars and devoted readers mined his voluminous letters, journals, and unpublished essays.

Summing up his life and witness, Merton remarked:

> My own peculiar task in my Church and in my world has been that of the solitary explorer who, instead of jumping on all the latest bandwagons at once, is bound to search to existential depths of faith in its silences, its ambiguities, and in those certainties which lie deeper than the bottom of anxiety. In those depths there are no easy answers, no pat solutions to anything. It is a kind of submarine life in which faith sometimes mysteriously takes on the aspect of doubt, when, in fact, one has to doubt and reject conventional and superstitious surrogates that have taken the place of faith. On this level, the division between Believer and Unbeliever ceases to be so crystal clear. It is not that some are all right and others all wrong: all are bound to seek in honest perplexity. Everybody is an Unbeliever more or less! Only when this fact is fully experienced, accepted, and lived with, does one become fit to hear the simple message of the Gospel—or any other religious teaching.[16]

For Merton, the modern spiritual crisis was largely a crisis of authenticity. The sheer omnipresence of the political-economic realm leads people to identify completely with their social selves and communal myths—so much so that they no longer experience the solitude necessary for an encounter with God and their own true selves. The way back to a spiritual life requires a shedding of all the false identifications foisted upon us by our own ambitions, our friends and family, politicians, advertisers, and religious ideologues. In *Zen and the Birds of Appetite,* Merton put it this way:

> The root of personality is to be sought in the "true Self" which is manifested in the basic unification of consciousness in which subject and ob-

16. Thomas Merton, *Faith and Violence* (Notre Dame, Ind.: University of Notre Dame Press, 1968), 213.

ject are one. Hence the highest good is "the self's fusion with the highest reality." Human personality is regarded as the force which effects this fusion. The hopes and desires of the external, individual self are all, in fact, opposed to this higher unity. They are centered on the affirmation of the individual. It is only at the point where the hopes and fears of the individual self are done away with and forgotten "that the true human personality appears." In a word, realization of the human personality in this highest spiritual sense is for us the good toward which all life is to be oriented.[17]

Given this view on the nature of reality, Merton exposed the conventional and superstitious surrogates for faith in order to bring the perennial wisdom of religious tradition to bear upon the crises of our time. He saw the modern world as ruled by a growing technological imperative—the principle that if something is technologically possible, it must be done. This abdication of moral responsibility struck him as symptomatic of our inability to think rationally about the tools that shape our lives and revealed the mythic role technological determinism plays as a surrogate "religious" value.

Merton was not against technology, but he worried about the human tendency to make too much of a good thing, to turn a means into an end, and a gift into an idol, thus putting technology directly under the values of the false self. He was also one of the first religious thinkers to seriously consider the spiritual effects of the mass media—particularly the false psychological environments it created and the addictions and illusions it fostered. He wrote:

Nine tenths of the news, as printed in the papers, is pseudo-news, manufactured events. Some days ten tenths. The ritual morning trance, in which one scans columns of newsprint, creates a peculiar form of generalized pseudo-attention to a pseudo-reality. This experience is taken seriously.

17. Thomas Merton, *Zen and the Birds of Appetite* (New York: New Directions, 1968), 69. Merton is quoting the Zen philosopher Kitaro Nishida here.

It is one's daily immersion in "reality." One's orientation to the rest of the world. One's way of reassuring himself that he has not fallen behind. That he is still there. That he still counts! My own experience has been that renunciation of this self-hypnosis, of this participation in the unquiet universal trance, is no sacrifice of reality at all. To "fall behind" in this sense is to get out of the big cloud of dust that everybody is kicking up, to breathe and to see a little more clearly.[18]

And yet even though he seldom prescribed direct answers to life's many difficulties, Merton did advocate prayer, silence, solitude, and recollection as medicines against modernity and antidotes for its attendant illusions.

All prayer, reading, meditation, and all the activities of the monastic life are aimed at *purity of heart,* an unconditional and totally humble surrender to God, a total acceptance of ourselves and of our situation as willed by Him. It means the renunciation of all deluded images of ourselves, all exaggerated estimates of our own capacity in order to obey God's will as it comes to us in the difficult demands of life in its exacting truth. *Purity of heart* is then correlative to a new spiritual identity—the "self" as recognized in the context of realities willed by God. Purity of heart is the enlightened awareness of the new man, as opposed to the complex and perhaps rather disreputable fantasies of the "old man."[19]

Merton worried that the wisdom of nonviolence as articulated by Jesus, Gandhi, and Martin Luther King would be vulgarized—not only by those who opposed it, but by those who acted in its name. So he sought to clarify its true significance in a number of essays and letters. For him it was a serious mistake to regard nonviolence simply as a novel tactic that enables the sensitive man to participate in the struggles of the world without being dirtied with blood. Nonviolence was not just a way

18. Merton, *Faith and Violence,* 151.
19. Thomas Merton, *Contemplative Prayer* (Garden City, N.Y.: Doubleday, 1971), 68. Emphasis in original.

of getting what one wants without being involved in behavior that one considers ugly and evil. To practice nonviolence for a purely selfish end would in fact discredit the truth of nonviolent resistance.

The hope of the Christian, Merton told us, must be like the hope of a child, pure and full of trust. The Christian, in his humility and faith, must be as totally available to his world as the child is. But he cannot see the world with childlike innocence and simplicity unless his memory is cleared of past evils by forgiveness, and his anticipation of the future is free of calculation through purity of intention. "The main difference between nonviolence and violence," Merton explains, "is that the latter depends entirely on its own calculations. The former depends entirely on God and on His word."[20]

And so we arrive again at the religious revelation that a shift in the axis of understanding must be achieved, and that the epistemological preoccupations of the old science must give way to the healing revelations of the contemplative mind.

Philosopher King

The new world must be built by resolute men who "when hope is dead will hope by faith"; who will neither seek premature escape from the guilt of history, nor yet call the evil, which taints all their achievements, good. There is no escape from the paradoxical relation of history to the kingdom of God. History moves towards the realization of the Kingdom but yet the judgment of God is upon every new realization.

Reinhold Niebuhr, *The Nature and Destiny of Man*[21]

What we ask from Christianity is not a narrow concern for personal salvation but a social ideal that will stir enthusiasm and gain our devotion.

20. Thomas Merton, *Passion for Peace: The Social Essays*, ed. William H. Shannon (New York: Crossroad, 1995), 257, 258.
21. Reinhold Niebuhr, *The Nature and Destiny of Man*, vol. 2. (New York: Charles Scribner's Sons, 1945 [1943]), 285–86.

Christianity must not give a warning to set one's face against this world but a vision of the worth and meaning of the work to be done in this life.

Robert Roth, *American Religious Philosophy*[22]

The medium, by which spirits understand each other, is not the surrounding air, but the freedom which they possess in common.

Samuel Taylor Coleridge[23]

Martin Luther King Jr. was a theologically conservative Baptist minister who was, nevertheless, avant-garde in his application of Christian principles to the social and economic injustices of his time. His prophetic witness coupled to his neoplebeian theology challenged the racial complacencies of the white American church and the residual racist attitudes of the entire nation. Moreover, King pushed the envelope of Reinhold Niebuhr's Christian realism, organizing the poor and inaugurating an era of Christian activism that formed a stark contrast to the militant extremism of Black Power advocates such as Stokely Carmichael and to the conservative quietism of the late-fifties middle class. As a result, King's short life of Christian witness was plagued by slander, FBI and IRS harassment, violence, and ultimately assassination.

To fathom his unique contribution to our time without sentimentalizing his struggle or reducing it to clichés requires that we consider what remains undigested and unabsorbed of his thought. If we are going to see him as a culture hero, we must value the visionary nature of his intentions over the immediacy of his results, for King, like Gandhi, saw himself as serving something greater than history. Call it justice, call it the kingdom of heaven, it stands over and above political expediency in its appeal to responsibilities that transcend our own immediate wants, needs, and commitments.

---

22. Robert J. Roth, S.J., *American Religious Philosophy* (New York: Harcourt, Brace & World, 1967), 10.

23. I. A. Richards, *Coleridge on Imagination* (London: Routledge & Kegan Paul, 1950), 98.

King's life was Shakespearean—not only in the sense that it was tragic and theatrical, but also in the sense that, like Shakespeare, he used typology and Midrash to interpret the Bible.[24] When he was twenty-six years old, King told those gathered at the first meeting of the Montgomery bus boycott, "If you will protest courageously, and with dignity and Christian love, when the history books are written in future generations, the historians will have to pause and say, 'There lived a great people—a black people—who injected new meaning into the veins of civilization.' This is our challenge and our overwhelming responsibility."[25] King believed that an energized and spiritualized black America in possession of its self-respect and committed to change could heal at the deepest ontological levels the diseased psyche of America and by so doing rock its pretenses to empire the same way the early Christians had once rocked Rome.

To do this, he would have to find the form, the language, and the will to mobilize this thirst for justice—even if the white majority of Americans refused to recognize the black American witness. King found the method for this struggle in Gandhian nonviolence, the language for it in the Bible, and the will to accomplish it in the just indignation of black Americans. But it was his particular gift to synthesize all three of these ingredients in his voice, a voice that shook the very foundations of the American conscience and revealed an "antipolitical politics" bubbling just under the surface of American postwar cynicism.

In the postwar setting, King's theme of the redemptive power of agape, the moral ecology of divine providence, the sacredness of the human personality, and the moral obligation to resist structures of oppression took on a peculiar prescience. It was as if what once appeared backward and parochial—rural black Christianity—turned out to be something larger than anyone had previously imagined. It emerged as a profound new understanding of the human will as a vehicle for social change.

24. See Steven Marx, *The Bible and Shakespeare* (New York: Oxford University Press, 2000).

25. Martin Luther King Jr., quoted in Vincent Harding, "Getting Ready for the Hero," *Sojourners* 15, no. 1 (Jan. 1986): 18.

This defense and "expression" of the deep self—forged as it was in struggles to redeem everyday life from the unconscious barbarism of racism—turned out to be the first public assault upon the new totalitarian impulses unleashed into the world as a result of World War II. Not that racism in the United States was a postwar phenomenon—but its mechanisms, its systematic brutality, and its ideology stood revealed as part and parcel of the fascist plague that had desecrated Europe and now threatened both the Soviet Union and the United States.

As a black man living in America, King could never forget that we are all born into a people, an ethnicity, a historical moment, and hence a *destiny*. For him much more was at stake in social policies than our national mood or economic interests. Our character and souls were reflected in the laws we wrote, defended, and obeyed. And so a public man had to live in a debt of gratitude to the people from which he emerged as a human being. He could not simply "make" policy according to his own intellectual lights—or those of the best and the brightest around him. Such "think-tank" politics could be creative, often even brilliant, but it was inevitably thin and historically superficial.

In Being's struggle with becoming, one finds oneself written, as it were, across the sky of historical change. And with an awareness of this comes the recognition that one's quest for meaning and dignity can be realized only by activating the will against the general will-less-ness. In other words, against the conditional life and the boredom of the good mind that acquiesces to it, doing God's will maintains the unconditional possibility against the technological mind that is always seeking the single best answer.

Reinhold Niebuhr had criticized Gandhi's attempt to introduce religion into politics by arguing that nonviolence was itself coercive—that it too could lead to violence—and that any attempt to collapse these two realms was impossible and only inflated Gandhi's power plays under the false pretenses of disinterested morality. In politics, Niebuhr argued, "love" was not possible, only the negative good of justice was possible—and one had to use power and coercion to enforce it. Humanity could not be persuaded to be selfless; its inherent selfishness—entrenched as it was in self-righteous collectivities—could be checked only by structures of power.

At first King accepted this view and saw the use of boycotts and mass demonstrations as an acknowledgment of the need for coercion to accompany moral suasion. But King's experiences in the movement gave him a glimpse of other human possibilities that Niebuhr's realism simply could not explain. King remarks:

> The experiences in Montgomery did more to clarify my thinking in regard to the question of nonviolence than all of the books that I had read. As the days unfolded, I became more and more convinced of the power of nonviolence. Nonviolence became more than a method to which I gave intellectual assent; it became a commitment to a way of life. Many issues I had not cleared up intellectually concerning nonviolence were now resolved within the sphere of practical action.[26]

Inside this remark are embedded all the profound emotional events of that first campaign—dealing with the anger, responding to the obfuscations and the pressure tactics, undergoing arrest, becoming a national figure, having his house bombed and his life threatened. Yet King was moving beyond Niebuhr's admission of the tactical usefulness of nonviolence within certain limited circumstances to embrace nonviolence *as a way of life*, as a way to transfigure himself and heal a nation caught in the tragic conflicts generated by its own racist past.

In a 1965 *Playboy* magazine interview, King mentioned how the bombing of the 16th Street Baptist Church in Birmingham, in which four little girls were murdered as they sat in their Sunday school class, confronted him once again with the issue that if men are this bestial, is it worth it? Is there any hope? Is there any way out? The interviewer asked, "Do you still feel this way?" King responded:

26. *The Strength to Love* (Philadelphia: Fortress, 1986), 151–52.

No, time has healed the wounds—and buoyed me with the inspiration of another moment which I shall never forget: when I saw with my own eyes over three thousand young Negro boys and girls, totally unarmed, leave Birmingham's 16th Street Baptist Church to march to a prayer meeting— ready to pit nothing but the power of their bodies and souls against Bull Connor's police dogs, clubs and fire hoses. When they refused Connor's bellowed order to turn back, he whirled and shouted to his men to turn on the hoses. It was one of the most fantastic events of the Birmingham story that these Negroes, many of them on their knees, stared, unafraid and unmoving, at Connor's men with the hose nozzles in their hands. Then slowly the Negroes stood up and advanced, and Connor's men fell back as though hypnotized, as the Negroes marched on past to hold their prayer meeting. I saw there, I felt there, for the first time the pride and the *power* of nonviolence.[27]

Nonviolence goes beyond the tragic awareness of Christian Realism to affirm an epiphanic realm counter to history, where God's will reveals itself in new, unimagined, and undreamed-of possibilities. It is as if in affirming the paradoxical clash of moral man against immoral society, King discovered the God of Apocalyptic Hope. "I AM WHO I WILL BE."[28]

This synthesis of essentialist theology with existential dialectics takes place in the street, in practice, in the struggle itself. It is not exactly the triumph of practical reason over theory so much as the recognition that certain limit conditions exposed by Niebuhr can sometimes be transcended by communities of faith resisting injustice. Such moments do not invalidate Niebuhr's sense of the paradox between the unconditioned soul and the conditional realms of history, but they do point the way to "the beloved community."

Besides, it's one thing to argue that one must temper one's utopian longings when one is resisting a fanatical popular movement such as

27. Martin Luther King, quoted in *Testament of Hope*, ed. James M. Washington (San Francisco: Harper & Row, 1986), 347.

28. For the connection of this phrase with liberation theology, see Dennis P. McCann, *Christian Realism and Liberation Theology* (Maryknoll, N.Y.: Orbis Books, 1982).

fascism or communism, but to voice such concerns in the United States in the fifties when no popular movements existed to check government-sanctioned racism or to direct public priorities toward populist ends is an entirely different thing. Niebuhr, who came of age in the thirties, just assumed the existence of a public in tension with its ruling structures—a populist culture pleading its own agenda and pushing at the seams of the systems that contained it. He didn't factor into his analysis a radical imbalance of power where the conformist masses acquiesced to their own political obsolescence. In such a context, Christian "realism" can all too easily become a pretext for sitting on one's hands.

Activists like Dorothy Day and Martin Luther King Jr. understood spiritual truths often reserved only for soldiers, firefighters, and the physically brave: namely, that courage deepens the silences, that putting one's body on the line for another can be a form of prayer, and that shared risk, like shared suffering, teaches us forms of humility, love, and compassion that are often too deep for words, incapable of being integrated into any rational political calculus or propaganda campaign.

The first time Martin Luther King Jr. walked across the Edmunds Pettis Bridge in Selma, Alabama, in 1965, toward those clubs and armed police officers, he—like everyone else on the bridge that day—was walking on faith, and it's impossible to say exactly what he learned that day about southern politics, nonviolence, or the way of the cross. I suspect even he couldn't articulate it. But one could see its impact in the changed quality of his conviction, in the tenor of his voice the next day, in the determination of his gait, and in his final fearlessness before death. It isn't that such experiences teach us to be heroic; it's more that they confront us with *what it really is that we are afraid of*—forcing us to come to grips with our attachments and self-centered misreading of what this life on earth is actually for.

Taylor Branch argues that King turned Niebuhr's philosophy on its head.[29] Niebuhr's doctrines argued that private virtue was possible, while

29. Taylor Branch, *Parting the Waters* (New York: Simon & Schuster, 1988), 702.

public virtue impossible, and yet King's experience in Montgomery had taught him the reverse lesson: he had performed a miracle of public virtue, and yet he was more aware than ever of his own personal capacity for sin. Personal evil seemed more intractable than social evil, contradicting the key thesis in Niebuhr's *Moral Man and Immoral Society.*

King's personalism and respect for religious mystery led him to sense the limitations of any essentialist theological anthropology—even one so wise as Niebuhr's. Any worldview that defined humanity before all the evidence of history was in was inherently suspect. For King, the search for a method was transformed into a nonviolent way of life. Alienation was evidence of frustrated communication, the product of segregation between races, between cultures, and even between aspects of the self. And agape was not a private psychological experience but a form of communication that could not exist in isolation from community. It found its highest expression in hospitality and service.

King's religious commitments, like Dorothy Day's, freed him from any Hegelian "will to a system." The foundation of his thought was not an idea, but a person and a set of images entering into dialogue with an uncertain, mysterious promise. The pragmatists' concerns with tactics and results was, for King, just more evidence of the incomplete philosophical analysis born of modernism—the amoral bent of a materialist mind cut off from the experience of human struggle and therefore incapable of grasping the full implications of the Word made flesh. In linking the civil rights movement with the peace movement, and the peace movement with the war on poverty, King intuited the possible emergence of a spiritual way of life for the masses no longer resigned to serving the needs of existing social structures, commerce, or government.

King believed that modern civilization had pried people away from their traditions, their families, and their spiritual desires. And so by linking the civil rights movement to the peace movement and to the moral destinies of all people, he sought to expose the bastardization of world culture hiding behind the name of global economic development.

The real enemy wasn't ignorant white bigots but the emerging world corporate system and its increasing disregard for the human person. To fight this hydra-headed monster, King advocated a well-formed interior life coupled with Gandhian activism. His vision demanded not only an engaged life, but a militant one, for his basic assumption was that our collective lives would not become more just unless they were compelled to be so, nor could our individual lives be humane unless purged from within by transformative spiritual practices.

I don't think it was a coincidence that King was planning a retreat with Thomas Merton the year they both died; both of these men felt a need to connect and to think through their shared notion that those on the bottom were the only ones with the power to heal the whole—not through armed rebellion but through their power to forgive. Those in power had to find the contrition of heart *to accept their forgiveness*. Those who profit from injustice must recognize their collusion with sin and do penance. And so by opening themselves to a relationship they have long denied, the powerful find moral direction—perhaps for the very first time.

This superiority of the oppressed over the oppressor is not a form of moral one-up-man-ship, but rather an insight into the psychological truth of things. It links the nonviolent revolutionary to a force greater than themselves, breaking the shackles of any residual sense of inferiority and thus makes possible a more powerful form of self-affirmation that unites rather than divides. King explains: "I think the greatest victory of this period was something internal. The real victory was what this period did to the psyche of the black man. The greatness of this period was that we armed ourselves with dignity and self-respect. The greatness of this period was that we straightened our backs up. And a man can't ride your back unless it's bent."[30]

The evil the enemy may do never expresses all that he is. This anthropology of hope is a wager not so much on the goodness of humanity as on its infinite complexity. It asserts that in the depths and turmoil of the

30. Coretta Scott King, ed., *The Words of Martin Luther King, Jr.* (New York: Newmarket Press, 1987 [1983]), 47.

inner life—that realm of the will that is by definition divided against itself—reside mysteries and potentialities beyond our self-descriptions. New regions within the enemy can be reclaimed—and they can become battlegrounds for the good. Grief and contrition can open new spaces in the heart—new avenues of reconciliation. Such is the expansive geography of the spiritual life, and the nonviolent front encompasses the entire terrain.

In seeking to redeem the enemy, not defeat him, King moves beyond the epic conceits of the warrior mythologies to a Christian critique of the triumphant self-over-others mythology. Echoing Simone Weil's analysis of *The Iliad,* he asserts that only those who know the glory of violent battle and *are not impressed by it* can truly bring about a new ethic on the far side of heroic individualism.

But fear often clouds our minds and obscures our best intentions. When you are the victim of injustice or the object of hatred, it is not always so easy to remember the lessons of the past, or even cling to common sense.

In his sermon "The Answer to a Perplexing Problem," King addresses the question of how evil might be cast out of our collective and individual lives. He rejects waiting on God, and he rejects taking history into our own hands. Instead, he articulates a third option: "Both man and God, made one in a marvelous unity of purpose through an overflowing love as the free gift of himself on the part of God and by perfect obedience and receptivity on the part of man, can transform the old into the new and drive out the deadly cancer of sin."[31]

To change the world we must become receptacles of God's love, understanding, and goodwill. We must have faith, not merely of the mind, but of the heart that surrenders the whole man to the divine inflow. This is a departure from Niebuhr's dualism, which admits a metanoia of the soul but not of community: in King's view, moral action links personal salvation directly to social responsibility. This is also a departure from progressive

31. Martin Luther King Jr., *Strength to Love* (Philadelphia: Fortress Press, 1986), 134.

liberalism, because it sets divine limits to change and to one's own capacity to effect change. Victory is not the goal—doing God's will is.

One sees here all the great themes of liberation theology—the primacy of persons over structures, a preference for the poor, a rejection of both individualism and collectivism for the participatory beloved community, and the moral obligation to resist collective evil. But there is also something that transcends even these values: King's Christian suspicion of any and all merely human enterprises, their easy corruptibility, and their all too human proclivity to devolve into systems and method.

If King had survived to witness the assassination of Robert Kennedy, and the subsequent disillusionments of Watergate, Contragate, the Reagan Revolution, Bush I, the Clinton years, and Bush II, I suspect he would not have despaired but would have interpreted these developments as the inevitable move of the pendulum of history back from a revolutionary time to an age of conservative retrenchment requiring even more pressure from the people against the growing marginality of their personhood. For King had always found his inspiration in the figure of the apostle Paul. Rejecting bitterness, resignation, and withdrawal, King advises us to take up the burden of our disappointments and by so doing transform them into challenges. "Our willing acceptance of unwanted and unfortunate circumstances even as we still cling to radiant hope, our acceptance of finite disappointment even as we adhere to infinite hope. This is not the grim, bitter acceptance of the fatalist, but the achievement found in Jeremiah's words, 'This is a grief, and I must bear it.'"[32]

As our actual collective lives wither, our imaginations turn to the exotic, and the mass media becomes even more spectacular and specious. The middle class reads self-help books in an effort to teach themselves how to more effectively turn their lives into commodities so as to overcome any residual personhood that might be holding them back from success. Reality-television-show contestants—bent on "survival" at any

32. Ibid., 90.

cost—actually turn themselves into objective correlatives of the new social Darwinism. Gone is our humanity and—as Allan Bloom once argued—gone are our humanities.[33] Yet King still stands as the dreamer, the challenging counterexample.

The great tragedy of King's life was to die before he could lead nonviolence into its next phase (a task that has been bequeathed to King's friend Thich Nhat Hanh and the Dalai Lama). But he did something, perhaps, even more important: he refused to let the American Transcendental Dream of radical democratic individualism die—even in the face of cold war militarism and Reinhold Niebuhr's compromise with power.

It often strikes me as odd that although the biographers can account for almost every hour of King's life—where he was and what he did—and sometimes even speculate as to the full dimensions of his courage, we have very little record of his spiritual joys. His close friend, the Reverend Abernathy, documented his vices, and his wife, Coretta, his family happiness, but if the modern Christian novelists have taught us anything about the life of the soul, it is that it cannot be encompassed by such quotidian realities, facts, or descriptions. The soul lives halfway outside of itself, looking down on everything with and through God.

Perhaps King's last speech, more than any other he ever gave, reveals to us what he saw unfolding before him as his destiny. But if that is so, then he truly left us having lived only half a life and, hence, half a prophecy. Those who wish to get closer to King's vision will have to undergo their own set of spiritual exercises and live for years with the contradictory facts of King's life. Perhaps only then might we begin to grasp why God demands always and only the impossible.

The King phenomenon—if we can call it that—was a miracle of responsibility. Perhaps it is still too early to measure his success because it is still being realized, but there is no doubt that he proved that it is possible to win back the sublimity of our religious traditions without abandoning

33. See Allan Bloom, *The Closing of the American Mind* (New York: Simon & Schuster, 1988).

our hard-won knowledge of their moral limitations. His life proves that we can refurbish the ladder of Being without capitulating either to the premodern vices of superstition, sentimentality, and self-righteous prejudice or to the postmodern vices of indifference, superficiality, cynicism, and moral paralysis.

E. F. Schumacher's Guide for the Perplexed

The Western world's loss of classical/Christian ethics has left us impoverished devotees of the religion of economic growth, heading for every conceivable kind of world disaster.

Victoria Brittain[34]

The modern experiment to live without religion has failed, and once we have understood this, we will know what our "post modern" tasks really are.

E. F. Schumacher, *A Guide for the Perplexed*[35]

E. F. Schumacher is really an apologetical preacher, one of the rare breed whose experience has made it possible for him to employ effectively the language and concepts of economics as a medium for communicating what is essentially a sermon, a call for readers to repent, believe the gospel and reorder their lives accordingly. Schumaucher himself insists that it is this "meta-economic" foundation of his argument that is most important, rather than the specifics of, say, his attacks on nuclear power or the use of chemicals in agriculture. "Everywhere people ask," he writes, 'What can I actually do?' The answer is as simple as it is disconcerting: we can, each of us, work to put our own inner house in order."

Charles Fager, *Christian Century*[36]

34. Quoted in Joseph Pearce, *Literary Converts: Spiritual Inspiration in an Age of Unbelief* (San Francisco: Ignatius Press, 1999), 376.
35. E. F. Schumacher, *A Guide for the Perplexed* (London: J. Cape, 1977), 139.
36. Charles Fager, "Small Is Beautiful, and So Is Rome: Surprising Faith of E. F. Schumacher," *Christian Century*, April 6, 1977, 325.

E. F. Schumacher converted to Catholicism in 1971, two years before
the publication of *Small Is Beautiful*. The chapter titled "Buddhist Economics" gives the impression that he embraced Eastern religions, but
the primary sources for his metaeconomic theory were the macrohis-
toricism of Thomas Aquinas, G. K. Chesterton's essays on distributism,
and Pope John XXIII's social encyclical *Mater et Magistra*.[37] Economics,
for Schumacher, was a derived science that took its instructions from
the very same philosophical and culture premises that shaped social life.
He chose to use Buddhism for his alternative metaeconomic model, but
he always admitted that the teachings of Christianity, Islam, or Judaism
could just as easily have been used to illustrate his point that when cultural
assumptions change, so do economic laws.[38] For example, the concept
of labor in the West is seen as a necessary evil—one of the "costs" of
production; whereas from a Buddhist perceptive, right livelihood is one
of the cornerstones of spiritual development. Labor doesn't just produce
goods; it offers an individual a chance to overcome egocentricism by bene-
fiting humanity. Soul-destroying work—no matter how cost-effective—is
counterproductive from a Buddhist point of view, producing unforeseen
social difficulties.

In his 1957 talk "The Insufficiency of Liberalism," Schumacher argued
that there were three stages of human development: first was primitive
religiosity, and then scientific realism. The third stage, which we are now
entering, is the realization that there is something beyond fact and science.[39] The problem, he explained, is that stage one and stage three look
the same to those in stage two. Consequently, those in stage three are
seen as having relapsed into magical thinking when, in reality, they have
actually seen through the limitations of rationalism. "Only those who
have been through stage two," he argues, "can understand the difference
between stage one and stage three."[40] That is to say, only those who have

37. Ibid., 366.
38. Ibid., 365.
39. Ibid., 366–67.
40. Ibid., 367.

come to realize the theoretical limitations inherent to instrumental logic understand the need for "metaeconomic" values.

"When we come to politics," Schumacher insisted, "we can no longer postpone or avoid the question regarding man's ultimate aim and purpose."[41] If one believes in God, one will pursue politics mindful of the eternal destiny of man and the truths of the gospel. However, if one believes that there are no higher obligations, it becomes impossible to resist the appeal of Machiavellianism: politics defined "as the gaining and maintaining of power so that you and your friends can order the world as they like."[42]

The purpose of education, according to Schumacher, is to help us clarify to ourselves the ideas we *think with;* that is to say, education should make us conscious of our convictions and assumptions so that the meaning of our experiences becomes less muddy. We don't think *ideas,* he tells us; we think *through ideas.* Concepts are the tools we use to sort, define, and comprehend the meaning of events. The ideas *we think with* are different from the ideas *we think.* The ideas we now typically think *with* were born largely in the nineteenth century and manifest themselves in two equally questionable sets of assumptions: (1) a scientific positivism that sees our highest good in doing away with metaphysics entirely in order to acquire "know-how" and (2) the late nineteenth century's version of "the humanities," born of vulgar appropriations of Marx and Freud, which reduce all human experiences to their social and psychological determinants. What both of these approaches have in common is a denial of any qualitative differences between facts or entities. They both collapse the old hierarchies in order to render life knowable in terms of its most basic elements.[43]

41. Ibid., 368.

42. Ibid., 368–69.

43. I find it interesting that the late French literary critic Roland Barthes described both Marx and Freud as *structuralists* and pointed out that later, more empirical scientists derided both of them for not being more reductive and materialist. For Barthes, this just goes to show that Marx and Freud were really *novelists!* Hence their continued influence on our time despite the failure of their "science."

Schumacher argues that this approach does not clarify anything; in fact, it constitutes, as Blake pointed out, a veritable "second fall of mankind." Reductionist approaches deny the very existence of a hierarchy of Being. They work only for problems that yield to convergent thinking—problem-solving strategies built upon the elaboration of systems. Convergent thinking takes you out of the world of complex interdependent realities into a single, independent order of thought where mathematical analyses can prevail—what Walker Percy would call "dyadic" or "cause-and-effect" forms of rationality.

Here the paradigm is natural science, with its stipulative definitions and its verifiable hypotheses. Problems that come from "the real world," Schumacher argues, do not yield to such reductionism. They usually demand a synthesis of irresolvable antinomies of some sort or another—such as freedom and order or security and risk—and this requires *divergent thinking*, that is to say, rule breaking, re-categorizing, and renaming kinds of processes so that we may rise to a more inclusive vision that synthesizes apparently irreconcilable oppositions into a higher conceptual unity. The divergent thinker is always "brainstorming."

The term *divergent thinking* was coined by J. P. Guilford, a psychologist well known for his research on creativity.[44] Guilford posited that a prime component of creativity is the capacity to arrive at unique and original solutions by considering problems in terms of multiple solutions. Convergent thinking narrows all options to one solution; it is orderly, step-by-step, and logical. Divergent thinking appropriates opposites. Conflicts between freedom and control in politics, for example, can be "solved" only by attaining to the higher level of "justice."

To the degree modern thought has sought to eliminate the very conception of a hierarchy of Being by reducing all things to their materiality, it has turned convergent thinking into an absolute, thus making ethical and philosophical problems increasingly difficult to solve—postponing them

---

44. See "Divergent Thinking" entry in *The Gale Encyclopedia of Childhood and Adolescence,* ed. Jerome Kagen (Detroit: Gale Research, 1998).

indefinitely until some new science can be developed that will reduce every variable to controllable, atomistic, material elements.

The hierarchy of Being, basic to any and all realist metaphysics, is an attractive alternative to scientific reductionism because it demands no leap of faith. A "higher" being in classical terms is simply an entity that includes all the attributes of the being "below" it but with one additional synthesizing element. The mineral kingdom is superceded by the plant kingdom only because vegetation is matter that can reproduce itself; the animal kingdom supersedes vegetative life by virtue of its synthesizing consciousness, and humanity supersedes animals by its awareness of itself as conscious.

If you deny qualitative differences, do away with the ladder of Being, and reduce all things to their lowest common denominator, you cannot solve complex problems—problems generated by the incompatibility of binary oppositions. Such problems have to be transcended via a more inclusive "logic." Perhaps this is what Einstein meant when he remarked that no problem in science can be solved at the same level of consciousness that created it.

Our nineteenth-century "antimetaphysical" assumptions claim to save us from superstition but don't provide us with creative solutions to any practical political or social problems; instead, they ship them off to various sciences divorced from practical life, sciences committed to the reduction of all things to their most basic operations. So we are told to wait until the "scientists" discover the "pill" that will make us happy or the technology that will make political compromise unnecessary and obsolete.

Schumacher sees this same deferral and lack of effectiveness in the inability of modern economics to come up with any solution for poverty. It simply cannot compute political disenfranchisement, ignorance, or cultural dysfunction into its materialist, industrially based equations. And when it tries, it has to abandon its claim to being a hard science. Only when it sticks to calculating profits and losses does economics lay any claim to mathematical precision; only when it ignores its own meta-economic commitments by sticking close to the assumptions it inherited from nineteenth-century scientism do we see any real number crunching.

Schumacher's critique of modern thought applied to economics exposes its reductionist principles, its questionable philosophical anthropology, its materialist metaphysics, its atomism, its impotence before the problems of the poor, its collusion with Western industrial models of development, its blindness to ecological issues, and its prejudices in favor of economies of scale, nationalistic politics, and globalization.

In his last book, *Guide for the Perplexed*, Schumacher extends his critique to life in general, demonstrating the continuing usefulness of the ladder of Being as a way of making important ontological and ethical distinctions. His analysis parallels in many ways that of Walker Percy's critique of contemporary semiology as well as René Girard's analysis of mimetic desire. (See the last section of chapter 4 in this book.) In all three cases, simple cause and effect is called into question by a third element. Schumacher's approach to economics helps to explain Helen Keller's "leap" into language as an ascension up the ladder of Being. Consciousness becomes "awareness" via metaphor, paradox, and irony, and a human being is born by participating in this collective naming of reality, however limited and prejudiced that "naming" might be.

Schumacher summarizes his views nicely at the conclusion of his *Guide for the Perplexed*:

1. One's first task is to learn from society and "tradition" and to find one's temporary happiness in receiving directions from outside.
2. One's second task is to interiorize the knowledge one has gained, sift it, sort it out, keeping the good and jettisoning the bad; this process may be called "individuation," becoming self-directed.
3. One's third task cannot be tackled until one has accomplished the first two, and is one for which one needs the very best help that can possibly be found: It is "dying to oneself," to one's likes and dislikes, to all one's egocentric preoccupations.

   To the extent that one succeeds in this, one ceases to be directed from outside, and also ceases to be self-directed. One has gained freedom or, one might say, one is then God-directed. If one is a

Christian, that is precisely what one would hope to be able to say. . . .
In order to become capable of loving and helping my neighbor as
well as myself, I am called upon to "love God," that is, strenuously
and patiently to keep my mind straining and stretching toward the
highest things, to Levels of Being above my own. Only there lies
"goodness" for me.[45]

Here is Schumacher's synthesis of Chesterton's economic "distributism"
with Walker Percy's view of the "self." We grow spiritually as individuals and ethically as citizens to the degree we welcome the problems of
everyday life as opportunities to overcome false antinomies by ascending
the ladder of Being.

So far the deeper cultural implications of Schumacher's thought have
not been fully appreciated by those who focus primarily upon the social
reforms advocated in *Small Is Beautiful*. But it is only a matter of time
until the full implications of his cultural critique are recognized and the
ecologists embrace the Great Chain of Being as a powerful, intellectual
tool.

Wendell Berry: Radical "Agrarian"

Industrialism prescribes an economy that is placeless and displacing. It
does not distinguish one place from another. It applies its methods and
technologies indiscriminately in the American East and the American
West, in the United States and in India. It thus continues the economy
of colonialism. The shift of colonial power from European monarchy to
global corporation is perhaps the dominant theme of modern history. All
along, it has been the same story of the gathering of an exploitive economic
power into the hands of a few people who are alien to the places and the
people they exploit. Such an economy is bound to destroy locally adapted
agrarian economies everywhere it goes, simply because it is too ignorant

45. Schumacher, *Guide for the Perplexed,* 149–50.

not to do so. And it has succeeded precisely to the extent that it has been able to inculcate the same ignorance in workers and consumers.

Wendell Berry, "The Agrarian Standard"[46]

Wendell Berry is an avant-garde writer only in the sense that his rural values have kept him rooted in a radical critique of modern industrialism and science—a critique that has become more and more pertinent over the years as the effects of modernity have become increasingly hard to ignore. Like the prophets of old, Berry sees a direct connection between the economy and the morale of the nation. You cannot replace family farmers with Wal-Mart employees without increasing the aimlessness and fear in society.

His solution, like that of Schumacher, G. K. Chesterton, Dorothy Day, and the "distributists," is to work for a greater distribution of private property across the board—encouraging family ownership of farms and small businesses while discouraging the accumulation of vast amounts of property and capital in the hands of the few. For Berry, this is not just an economic program but a moral imperative. Unless constrained by moral vision, institutions will always move in the direction of power and self-preservation, not high principle.

Industrialism, he believes, is the chief culprit here. It begins with technological invention, thus elevating change to a social priority; whereas agrarianism begins with land, plants, animals, weather, and hunger, thus giving priority to stability and civil order.

Industrialists are always ready to ignore, sell, or destroy the past in order to gain the entirely unprecedented wealth, comfort, and happiness supposedly to be found in the future. Agrarian farmers know that their very identity depends on their willingness to receive gratefully, use responsibly, and hand down intact an inheritance, both natural and cultural, from the past. The industrial economy thus is inherently violent. It impoverishes one

46. Wendell Berry, "The Agrarian Standard," *Orion,* Summer 2002–2003.

place in order to be extravagant in another, true to its colonialist ambition. A part of the "externalized" cost of this is war after war.[47]

In other words, industrialists move away from the local and particular to the general and the abstract, which is for Berry the great error of modern civilization. It abstracts individuals from their own one-of-a-kind lives and environments and divides them into competing communities; whereas a focus upon the particulars of life—this man, this woman, this land, and this project—promotes local economies and the values of specific communities. This is more effective on a small scale and leads to tolerance and cooperation on the large scale. A community economy is not an economy in which well-placed persons can make a killing, but an economy whose aim is generosity and a well-distributed and safeguarded abundance.

Berry's recent essay "Thoughts in the Presence of Fear" contains twenty-seven observations occasioned by the terrorist assaults against the United States. He remarks:

> The time will soon come when we will not be able to remember the horrors of September 11 without remembering also the unquestioning technological and economic optimism that ended on that day. This optimism rested on the false proposition that we were living in a "new world order" and a "new economy" that would "grow" on and on, bringing a prosperity of which every new increment would be "unprecedented." The dominant politicians, corporate officers, and investors who believed this proposition did not acknowledge that the prosperity was limited to a tiny percentage of the world's people, and to an ever smaller number of people even in the United States; that it was founded upon the oppressive labor of poor people all over the world; and that its ecological costs increasingly threatened all life, including the lives of the supposedly prosperous. The "developed" nations had given to the "free market" the status of a god, and were sacrificing to it their farmers, farmlands, and communities,

47. Wendell Berry, *Another Turn of the Crank* (New York: Counterpoint, 1996), 19–21.

their forests, wetlands, and prairies, their ecosystems and watersheds. They had accepted universal pollution and global warming as normal costs of doing business.[48]

Berry goes on to offer admonitions for ecological responsibility and the equitable distribution of wealth through widespread private and community ownership of businesses and farms. Then he sets out to describe what he sees as the socioeconomic and moral crossroads at which we have arrived.

> We now have a clear, inescapable choice that we must make. We can continue to promote a global economic system of unlimited "free trade" among corporations, held together by long and highly vulnerable lines of communication and supply, but now recognizing that such a system will have to be protected by a hugely expensive police force that will be worldwide, whether maintained by one nation or several or all, and that such a police force will be effective precisely to the extent that it oversways the freedom and privacy of the citizens of every nation.
>
> Or we can promote a decentralized world economy which would have the aim of assuring to every nation and region a local self-sufficiency in life-supporting goods. This would not eliminate international trade, but it would tend toward a trade in surpluses after local needs had been met.[49]

We stand, Berry tells us, at a turning point in history, and whichever road we take will define our lives from here on out. Will we take the road of empire or the road of democracy? Will we chose freedom for the few or freedom for the many? Will we make our lives more impersonal, global, abstract, and artificial or more intimate, local, connected, and authentic? Will we put our trust in machines or in people? In calculation or in revelation? Will we defend our families or the powers that be?

48. Wendell Berry, *Citizenship Papers* (Washington, D.C.: Shoemaker & Hoard, 2003), 17. "Thoughts in the Presence of Fear" first appeared in OrionOnline.org on September 24, 2001, in the Web magazine *Orion*. The entire article is reprinted in the Nonviolence Forum (www.forusa. org/nonviolence/w/Berry-thoughts.html)

49. Ibid., 19.

In a recent introduction to a new edition of *The Unsettling of America,* Berry laid out the conflict in a way that makes "industrialism" as much of a villain as Berdyaev made the "bourgeoisie."

> I believe that this contest between industrialism and agrarianism now defines the most fundamental human difference, for it divides not just two nearly opposite concepts of agriculture and land use, but also two nearly opposite ways of understanding ourselves, our fellow creatures, and our world. The way of industrialism is the way of the machine. To the industrial mind, a machine is not merely an instrument for doing work or amusing ourselves or making war; it is an explanation of the world and of life. Because industrialism cannot understand living things except as machines, and can grant them no value that is not utilitarian, it conceives of farming and forestry as forms of mining; it cannot use the land without abusing it.[50]

The "cutting-edge" thinkers in science, business, education, and politics, Berry insists, have no interest in the local knowledge that makes people native to the land and therefore good caretakers of their unique places. From the beginning, industrialism has driven people from their homes, shifting the economic function of the household from production of wealth for the family to the consumption of purchased goods from corporations. As a result, problems correctable on a small scale have been replaced by large-scale problems for which there are no solutions. Local farmers are forced to conform to the economic conditions imposed by an international market that has caused problems on the largest possible scale, including soil loss, genetic impoverishment, and groundwater pollution. These problems can be eliminated by an agriculture of locally adapted, solar-powered, diversified small farms—a correction that, after a half century of industrial agriculture, will be difficult to achieve.

The world economy, Berry argues, is now in a state of continuing crisis. It is threatened by the superstitions of "globalism" and "progress,"

50. Ibid. 144.

which reduce particular communities to mere factors in large-scale policy models. Blake's worst fears have now been realized, Goethe's warnings completely ignored, and Chesterton's insights lost on the "true believers" in technological progress who are themselves blissfully unaware of the Hegelian and Kantian categories they have swallowed with their Starbucks coffee.

"Legitimate faith in scientific methodology," Berry writes, "seems to veer off into a kind of religious faith in the power of science to know all things and solve all problems, whereupon the scientist may become an evangelist and go forth to save the world."[51] They then reduce everything to a mechanism that oversimplifies everything into "assemblages of perfectly featureless 'ecosystems,' 'organisms,' 'environments,' 'mechanisms' and the like." A morally complex view of the world cannot survive such abstract simplicities. To understand particular humans in particular situations, we need to cultivate an awareness of our ignorance of localities. It is dangerous to act on the assumption that every person and culture is essentially the same.

Berry extends his criticisms to the realm of contemporary politics, where millions of people end up suffering due to the miscalculations of the few. There is a kind of economic calculus that is invoked by the apologists for war that equates death with payment. We are told that the Union dead paid the ultimate price for the emancipation of the slaves and the preservation of the Union. And there is truth to this claim in that our freedom has been "paid for" by the sacrifices of others and that it would wrong for us not to be grateful. Extreme sacrifices must be made for the sake of liberty. But Berry is suspicious of the ease with which such accountings are perpetually invoked.

For one reason, it is necessarily done by the living on behalf of the dead. And I think we must be careful about too easily accepting, or being too easily grateful for, sacrifices made by others, especially if we have made

51. Wendell Berry, *Life Is a Miracle* (Washington, D.C.: Counterpoint, 2000), 18.

none ourselves. For another reason, though our leaders in war always assume that there is an acceptable price, there is never a previously stated level of acceptability. The acceptable price, finally, is whatever is paid. It is easy to see the similarity between this accounting of the price of war and our usual accounting of "the price of progress." We seem to have agreed that whatever has been (or will be) paid for so-called progress is an acceptable price. If that price includes the diminishment of privacy and the increase of government secrecy, so be it. If it means a radical reduction in the number of small businesses and the virtual destruction of the farm population, so be it. If it means the devastation of whole regions by extractive industries, so be it. If it means that a mere handful of people should own more billions of wealth than is owned by all of the world's poor, so be it.[52]

In the place of acquiescence to such worldwide injustice, Berry argues that national defense should be founded upon regional economic independence. We should be prepared to live from our own resources—not be dependent upon unstable alliances or other nations' resources or labor. But we are squandering our natural and human resources. There is no long-term energy, agriculture, or conservation plan.

Berry has developed seventeen rules for the preservation of ecological diversity and integrity, and renewal, on the ecological principles of local communities:

1. Always ask of any proposed change or innovation: What will this do to our community? How will this affect our common wealth?
2. Always include local nature—the land, the water, the air, the native creatures—within the membership of the community.
3. Always ask how local needs might be supplied from local sources, including the mutual help of neighbors.

52. Berry, *Citizenship Papers*, 26.

4. Always supply local needs first (and only then think of exporting products—first to nearby cities, and then to others).

5. Understand the ultimate unsoundness of the industrial doctrine of "labor saving" if that implies poor work, unemployment, or any kind of pollution or contamination.

6. Develop properly scaled value-adding industries for local products to ensure that the community does not become merely a colony of national or global economy.

7. Develop small-scale industries and businesses to support the local farm and/or forest economy.

8. Strive to supply as much of the community's own energy as possible.

9. Strive to increase earnings (in whatever form) within the community for as long as possible before they are paid out.

10. Make sure that money paid into the local economy circulates within the community and decrease expenditures outside the community.

11. Make the community able to invest in itself by maintaining its properties, keeping itself clean (without dirtying some other place), caring for its old people, and teaching its children.

12. See that the old and young take care of one another. The young must learn from the old, not necessarily and not always in school. There must be no institutionalized "child care" and no "homes for the aged." The community knows and remembers itself by the association of old and young.

13. Account for costs now conventionally hidden or "externalized." Whenever possible, these must be debited against monetary income.

14. Look into the possible uses of local currency, community-funded loan programs, systems of barter, and the like.

15. Always be aware of the economic value of neighborly acts. In our time, the costs of living are greatly increased by the loss

of neighborhood, which leaves people to face their calamities
alone.

16. A rural community should always be acquainted with, and com-
plexly connected with, community-minded people in nearby towns
and cities.

17. A sustainable rural economy will depend on urban consumers loyal
to local products. Therefore, we are talking about an economy that
will always be more cooperative than competitive.[53]

Here we see, in a nutshell, Berry's critique of the sacred cows of globalism and progress: Globalism is the vulgar popularization of Enlightenment philosophical universalism: the heady ambition to conquer life
itself through protean philosophical generalizations: universal theories
of humanity and global systems of commerce. Globalism breeds intellectual hubris, social hierarchies, oligarchies, and ultimately war. The
myth of "progress" justifies these things through the irrational belief
that they are necessary stages in the creation of a better world. This is
little more than a materialist version of pie-in-the-sky-by-and-by. The
present is sacrificed to the future, the truth of the present replaced by a
technoscientific utopian fantasy that has about as much chance of being
realized as the thousand-year Reich.

Such criticisms, of course, are not incredibly "original" formulations,
but what makes Berry's social criticism unique is that he carries it out
with a rigor and sophistication few other social ecologists can muster.
This is due, in part, to his Christian commitment to the particularism and
localism of the incarnation. The sacredness of life is always the sacredness of *this* life, *this* man or *this* woman—never in the abstract aggregate.
He brings this point home again and again: what we really want are not
labor-saving devices, but meaningful labor, what we really desire is not
empire but self-rule, not comfort but integrity, not power but freedom
and connection, and what will really set us free is not the license to do

---

53. Berry, *Another Turn of the Crank*, 19–22.

whatever we please but autonomy within community. To accomplish this, we do not need to martyr ourselves but to live and to sacrifice for our family and friends in simple harmony with nature.

Why is this so difficult?

4

Macrohistorical Criticism

After Hiroshima it was obvious that the loyalty of science was not
to humanity but to truth—its own truth—and that the law of sci-
ence was not the law of the good . . . but the law of the possible . . .
what it is possible for technology to do technology will have done.

Achibald MacLeish, "The Great American Frustration"[1]

With the growth of populous societies, the accumulation of wealth,
the development of complex political and religious establishments
and above all with the expansion of invention and resources for
war, human life on earth was revolutionized. That revolution began
with what we call "history" and has reached its climax now in an-
other and far greater revolution which may, in one way or other,
bring us to the end of history. Will we reach that end in cataclysmic
destruction or—as others affably promise—in a "new tribalism," a
submersion of history in the vast unified complex of mass-mediated

1. Archibald MacLeish, "The Great American Frustration," *Saturday Review,* July 13, 1968,
13–17.

relationships which will make the entire world one homogeneous
city? Will this be the purely secular, technological city, in which all
relationships will be cultural and nature will have been absorbed in
techniques? Will this usher in the millennium? Or will it be noth-
ing more than the laborious institution of a new kind of jungle,
the electronic labyrinth, in which tribes will hunt heads among the
aerials and fire escapes until somehow an eschatological culture
of peace emerges somewhere in the turbulent structure of artifice,
abstraction and violence which has become man's second nature?

Thomas Merton, *Ishi Means Man*[2]

Christian thinkers have always championed macrohistorical narratives like the Bible. From Augustine's *City of God* to Arnold Toynbee's twelve-volume *Study of History,* they have emphasized the incongruity between the values of civilization and those of the beloved community. Looking at larger historical patterns, they see a series of states evolving into republics and republics into empires. Toynbee, for example, saw the West moving toward a new globalized world order that was only the temporary vehicle for the development of a worldwide spirituality synthesizing Buddhism with Christianity. He warned that American citizens would gladly forfeit their republic for the heady promise of empire, and he worried that the United States itself was probably only a way station in the movement toward a new world order that would redefine all opposition to its international hegemony as "irrelevant."

Antonio Negri and Michael Hart's *Empire* expresses this same idea, only with the Marxist twist that this new superstate is actually the product of runaway idealism that needs to be overcome by a new political empiricism. The Christian social critics examined here again reverse this procedure, arguing that Christianity has been misrepresented and appropriated by the powers that be into a staid and static defense of existing institutions that hyperspiritualize its message and encourage an abstract, ahistorical, apocalyptic reading of Scripture.

2. Thomas Merton, *Ishi Means Man* (Greensboro, N.C.: Unicorn Press, 1976), 70, 71.

In this sense, organized religion, as Jesus, Paul, and Blake so well knew, is often the handmaiden of those in power; whereas the Christian revelation announced in Paul's letters and the Sermon on the Mount exposes this collusion of state with superstition by deconstructing the mythology of the scapegoat in all its guises. The Nobel Prize-winning poet Czeslaw Milosz compared what happened to Christianity in the West to taking the wrong subway train in New York. "You can go in a wrong direction somewhere. You go very far and can't get off. Maybe we've been on the wrong train. Goethe had an intuition that something was going wrong, that science should not be separated from poetry and imagination. Blake also."[3]

Perhaps we are beginning the return to a time when poetry, revelation, and the imagination can work alongside science. Reason alone no longer defines the horizon of our shared collective knowledge, and we have come to accept the fact that belief, commitment, revelation, even prayer, have a power to shape and revivify our lives, and that we cannot discount the presence of "the other" in our search for truth, nor can we ignore the "Other of the Other" without seriously undermining the objectivity of our analyses. God has found his way back into our epistemological deliberations for better or for worse. Rationalists can no longer flinch from Kierkegaard's argument that faith requires "a suspension of the ethical," because so does science, and so does business, and so does virtually every other autonomous discipline and practice.

What we need now is a criticism of these disciplines from within, an internal dissent, not from *their irrationality,* but from their wrongheadedness, their bogus inclusiveness, their willful blindness to others, and their narrow focus upon system. This was partially provided to us when Solzhenitsyn trumped Sartre's *Critique of Dialectical Reason* with *The Gulag Archipelago* and when Auden did the same thing to Heidegger's return to fundamental ontology with his return to biblical prophecy in *The Age of Anxiety.* The "new" Christian culture, in other words, is already here—has been for many years, but it's hidden from view by the fog of popular "religion," with its

3. Nathan Gardels, "An Interview with Czeslaw Milosz," *New York Review of Books* 33 (Feb. 27, 1986): 35.

specious evangelists, bad television shows, false controversies, and cyclical nonrevivals.

To fully grasp the meaning of these developments, we need to reinstate the distinction between our true and false selves, between our social identities and our souls, between the Christian culture that forms the metaphysical basis of the civilization we live in and the various misinterpretations of that tradition that make up popular faith. We need to distinguish between the political realities that shape our lives and the media version of "politics" that is little more than a form of mass entertainment and distraction. Much more has happened to us over the last twenty-five years than the rise of the West Coast business lobby in the eighties, the return of the East Coast Establishment in the nineties, or the 9/11 terrorist attacks. And yet an amazed public hears of little else as it watches on helplessly as would-be Caesars develop new technologies for Old Money and settle old scores with fresh blood.

Marshall McLuhan: The Christian in the Electronic Age

> As for Blake, McLuhan is his successor over and over again.
> George Steiner, *McLuhan: Hot and Cool*[4]

It is not brains or intelligence that is needed to cope with the problems which Plato and Aristotle and all of their predecessors to the present have failed to confront. What is needed is a readiness to undervalue the world altogether. This is only possible for a Christian. All technologies and all cultures, ancient and modern, are part of our immediate expanse. There is hope in this diversity since it creates vast new possibilities of detachment and amusement at human gullibility and self-deception. There is no harm in reminding ourselves from time to time that the "Prince of this World" is a great P.R. man, a great salesman of new hardware and software, a great electric engineer, and a great master of the media. It is his master stroke to

4. In *McLuhan: Hot and Cool*, Gerald Emmanuel Stearn, ed. (New York: New American Library, 1967), 234.

be not only environmental but invisible, for the environmental is invincibly persuasive when ignored.

Marshall McLuhan[5]

Too few of his readers realize that Marshall McLuhan's entire oeuvre is built upon a contemplative Christian worldview. A Catholic convert, McLuhan attended mass every week of his adult life and considered his radical theories and "thought experiments" as carrying Chesterton's use of irony into higher metaphysical levels—transforming paradox into "a genuine poetic instrument for creating worlds of discovery." The worlds of discovery that interested McLuhan, however, were interior worlds, changing sensoriums, and somatic readjustments. His "probes," as he called them, were pithy, epigrammatic "theories in miniature" designed to offer free and independent observations untethered to causal chains of thought or traditional linear arguments. He saw himself, therefore, more as an artist and theorist than as an intellectual systematizer.

McLuhan explains:

I'm perfectly prepared to scrap any statement I ever made about any subject once I find that it isn't getting me into the problem. I have no devotion to any of my probes as if they were sacred opinions. I have no proprietary interest in my ideas and no pride of authorship as such. You have to push any idea to an extreme, you have to probe. Exaggeration, in the sense of hyperbole, is a major artistic device in all modes of art. No painter, no musician ever did anything without extreme exaggeration of a form or a mode, until he had exaggerated those qualities that interested him. Wyndham Lewis said: "Art is the expression of a colossal preference" for certain forms of rhythm, color, pigmentation, and structure. The artist exaggerates fiercely in order to register this preference in some material. You can't build a building without huge exaggeration or preference for a certain kind of space.[6]

5. Marshall McLuhan, from a letter to Robert J. Leuver, quoted in *Marshall McLuhan: Escape into Understanding,* by W. Terrence Gordon (New York: Basic Books, 1997), 222–23.
6. Stearn, *McLuhan: Hot and Cool,* 277.

McLuhan understood that nothing is knowable independent from the environment that serves as its field. And every medium, like every form, privileges one sense, one space, one color, one reality over another, thereby shaping our experience of the world into very specific patterns. Print, for example, translates experience into linear classifications that coalesce into a "point of view."

Thus, in a print-oriented society, thought is the consistent ordering of things; whereas in preliterate cultures shaped by speech, experience is translated into sound and so words coalesce in the "presence" of the speaker. "Thought" in an oral culture is not the consistent ordering of things so much as it is a wisdom born of poetic naming. So when Western civilization shifted from an oral culture to print after the Gutenberg revolution, intellectual authority shifted from the wise man with experience and character to the expert equipped with logic and method. And there, for McLuhan, resides the essential conflict within Western intellectual history over the last four hundred years.

McLuhan believed that we were currently in the midst of yet another global transition from print to electronic media. This transition was bringing about a return of oral culture at the very moment computers had turned linear logic and calculative reason into a virtual God, thereby causing confusion in our understanding of ourselves and the way we process information. A generation gap was emerging on a global scale as the largely literate, educated classes came into conflict with the new orally oriented techno-peasants of the mass media. This was leading to a crisis in existing institutions between the new primitivism and the old hierarchies. On the one hand, the visual linear print culture constituted the rational, rule-based "establishment," and on the other, the new oral culture of interior experience made up its emotional, charismatic "counterculture" opposition.

McLuhan's willingness to explore the impact of these psycho-environmental changes made him one of the few modern Christian intellectuals interested in the new cultural forms emerging among the outsiders and avant-garde, not just in terms of their religious content but in terms of the shifting psychological fields and sensorial grids reshaping human consciousness across the world. McLuhan felt that it was important for scholars to explore the formal dimension to internal dissent and radical rebellion since no one raised in "the culture of the book" seemed to be taking these developments seriously. He predicted, for example, that the new media would give birth to a rise in illiteracy rates and a growth in political and religious extremism. His predictions were generally laughed off at the time, because then illiteracy rates had been declining for over fifty years and terrorism seemed a waning tactic on an increasingly enlightened world scene. But looking back, his predictions were not only accurate, but prophetic.

Donald Theall in his book *The Virtual McLuhan* describes McLuhan's unique relationship to contemporary cultural developments:

> McLuhan moved into exploring technology and culture because of his commitment to preserving a world in which a man of letters could assume authority through authoring essays and books that demonstrate "Change is dangerous and threatening." In pursuing the real relevance of McLuhan to the digital millennium, it is necessary to keep in mind his multi-schizoid orientation with its dislike of technology and change, its Nietzschean underside, its Catholic pietism, and its penetrating understanding of how the traditional domain of the artist and the humanities (in contradistinction to the humanist) was the crucial guide to understanding techno-culture.[7]

McLuhan himself wrote:

> The Wild Broncos of technological culture have yet to find their busters or masters. They have found only their P. T. Barnums. The future masters of technology will have to be lighthearted and intelligent. The machine easily masters the grim and the dumb.[8]

So although orthodox in his religious beliefs and traditional in his humanist commitments, McLuhan was avant-garde in his understanding of

7. Donald Theall, *The Virtual McLuhan* (Montreal and Kingston: McGill-Queens University Press, 2001), 50.

8. Marshall McLuhan, *Counter Blast* (New York: Harcourt, Brace & World, 1969), 54–55.

contemporary civilization and experimental in his methods for disclosing the hidden dynamics reshaping world civilization. In this sense, he was, as many have charged, a Christian apologist disguised as a media theorist, and his orthodoxy can be seen in his decidedly apocalyptic, but dispassionate, look across the entire expanse of world history.

Unlike Hegel and Marx, however, he didn't see a progression so much as a panorama of shifting technologies of consciousness. New media created new psychosocial environments that shape how we live, act, and think. Genres, modes, and all manner of literary and cultural forms work with these different modes of being to create perceptual worlds. "Myth," McLuhan explains, is "the mode of simultaneous awareness of a complex group of causes and effects."[9] It shapes perception, meaning, and sense in a single narrative structure. Thus, intellectual history as the history of consciousness is constantly recalibrating itself, not just in terms of some single metanarrative march of "reason" and/or "science" but in the evolution of its mythic and sensorial forms that generate human worlds within which life's meaning and purpose take shape.

The meaning of a work of art has to do with its action upon you—the way it restructures your outlook and changes your attitude. For McLuhan, the new electronic media were complex forms, and so their effect upon us was that of forms, not concepts. Particular media released a part of that inexhaustible store of analogical intuition and experience that made up human imaginative capacity, and so television and radio released a slew of experiences and intelligibilities that had lain dormant for centuries.

Unlike sociologically oriented critics, however, McLuhan relied upon the philological tools of etymology and exegesis because he believed that we could understand the products of the emerging new electronic culture only by grasping them as expressions of "new languages." And to do this, he needed to develop a grammar of mediated forms. This was the only way to articulate what our previous analyses had overlooked, namely, *the mediated*

---

9. Marshall McLuhan and Quentin Fiore, *The Medium Is the Message* (New York: Simon & Schuster, 1967), 114.

field within which the "content" of our lives was expressed. For McLuhan the so-called crisis of faith brought about by modernity was really more the result of a shift in primary media than any great epistemological calamity or "death of God."

The phonetic alphabet, he explained, had released the Greeks from the acoustic spell of tribal societies. The emotional detachment created by the written page gave them the power of the second look and therefore the capacity for reflection—freeing them from an uncritical and emotionally bound existence. This world of individual insight and private interior existence is now being destroyed by the new electronic media where "hearing is believing." And this is causing all kinds of confusions, especially in Third World countries that never experienced literacy in the first place, and so find their cultures torn in two by a barbarian "avant-garde" that is media-savvy, violent, emotional, aural, and mystical, and a traditionally "educated" conservative hierarchy that is more reasonable, but old-fashioned—that is to say, without charisma or passionate intensity.

Now that everyone in the world watches everyone else instantaneously, you can't tell the difference between the actors and the audience, combatants and civilians, reality and simulation. Indeed, McLuhan notes, the differences have all but vanished. The key to understanding modernity for those of us living at the speed of light is to realize that all experience has now become simultaneous and apprehended by the right side of our brains, whereas formerly experience had been sequential and logical and understood by the left hemisphere.

As a result, the religious universe of young people (like that of illiterate or preliterate societies) is something quite different from that of the literate church leadership. Today we are all much less interested in, or conflicted by, doctrinal or dogmatic disputes and far more open to experiential, even mystical, elements of the faith. We have very little difficulty imagining simultaneous, overlapping realities. The doctrine of the Trinity, once a conundrum, is now easily conceived and taken for granted.

Under electronic conditions, McLuhan tells us, we are liberated from natural law and find our ground in supernatural laws and experiences.

We are living in a global village characterized by the collective demystification of clashing world mythologies. Gone are the old Enlightenment certainties, as radical new sciences redefine everything, and the mass media commercializes and eliminates our fading Romantic illusions. Postliterate man turns out to be just as primitive, tribal, confused, and reactionary as McLuhan predicted he would be: "The West is going East—tribal and inward—The East is detribalizing—going West and outward—All identity images, private and corporate, dissolve, and a violent struggle to reign in these images ensues."[10]

Therefore, the crisis of postmodern civilization manifests itself as a crisis of identity for individuals on both sides of the generation gap and the world-historical divide. In the West, the vanishing point of Renaissance painting has been reversed, and it is our television sets that now look back at us. Camp, kitsch, and dreck—once symptoms of aesthetic decadence—have now become the everyday content of popular culture: a culture that has outpaced not only reality, but its own reflection of reality. Recently, one of the contestants on the game show *Survivor* declared that his fifteen days playing the game was "the most essential human experience of his life," testing his mettle and defining his true nature more profoundly than any other experience.

McLuhan provides us with a theory for understanding how "simulated" experience can take on such existential significance. Now all the world's mythologies stand revealed as products of one set of sensory modes (and hence one set of virtues and perceptions) over another; the electronic media retrieve certain lost, archaic energies but threaten to lose touch with those energies brought to the forefront by visual civilization. History now stands revealed as a multilayered, multifaceted value retrieval system functioning within a maelstrom of perceptual relationships moving in and out of one another through time, but getting nowhere. *Culture* has become a word social scientists use to describe the latest configuration of the mythic meanings indigenous to a specific geohistorical location; whereas *politics* is the

10. Marshall McLuhan, *Culture Is Our Business* (New York: McGraw Hill, 1970), 66.

word we now use to describe the hopeless attempt to remythologize our collective lives.

The relatively recent publication of McLuhan's letters has furthered our understanding of the spiritual dimension of his thought.[11] He was clearly trying to break through to higher philosophical ground in a cultural environment where big ideas were becoming an endangered species. He sensed the anti-intellectual, indeed antitheoretical, wave of the future, and so he designed his probes as poetic hypotheses: first steps toward a more inclusive vision of the whole. Add to his work the insights of other macrohistorical Christian thinkers such as René Girard, Jacques Ellul, and Ivan Illich, the focus tightens, and the spiritual peculiarities of our time are easier to see—preparing the way for an even more inclusive Christian anthropology than anything McLuhan himself had imagined.

Jacques Ellul explained in his book *Propaganda* that ideological indoctrination works best with a phonetically literate population.[12] The attention span of the electronically conditioned is insufficient for a complete psychological transformation. Likewise, the power of retention of those raised electronically is also diminished. And so any lasting cultural movement simply cannot take place in an electronic media environment. Postmodern fanaticism is, by its very nature, unstable, short-lived, and dangerously fluid. We are living in an age of momentary passions, improvised collectives, spur-of-the-moment convictions contradicted by spur-of-the-moment retractions.

In such a world, we need a strategy that can fuse the old and obliterated truisms with trite and current concerns—a way of bringing together the new and the surprising with the ancient and the timeless. Contemporary Christians do not live so much in a time of exile as in a time of instant and perpetual restoration. Therefore, they face the double-sided problem of letting go of their past without losing themselves in the instabilities of the

---

11. Marshall McLuhan, *Letters of Marshall McLuhan,* comp. and ed. Matie Molinaro and William Toye (Toronto: Toronto University Press, 1987).

12. Jacques Ellul, *Propaganda* (New York: Vintage Press, 1973), 2.

new Philistine civilization. This requires thinking through the relationship between liturgy and the new media.

Christian liturgy, McLuhan explains, is a form of communication fundamentally different from either drama or rhetoric, and if it's a ritual, it's ritual transcending itself. To incorporate modern means of expression, such as film or video or rock music into its structure, requires a deep and thorough understanding of both the meaning of liturgy and the new forms. You can't just "rap" the homily and expect to make your sermon contemporary, just as rock versions of hymns do not make contemplation accessible to teens.

Electric media, McLuhan tells us, are "inner trips" and so they tend to favor depth involvement in meditational forms. As a result, one would expect that today's faithful, educated by the new media, would prefer prayer and contemplative practices over sermons, as we can see in the surprising success of the Centering Prayer movement and new attention given to retreats and private spiritual direction. Moreover, as time and space shrink due to electric communication, denominations cease to matter as much, the place of worship becomes increasingly arbitrary, and ecumenism becomes an obvious need. Doctrinal disputes become battles between the old and new schools, between a literate, rational, uncharismatic past and an emotional, intuitive, future-oriented "present." Of course, both sides miss the larger picture of the clash of media that constitutes the true content of their disputes, so neither side is really right: they each represent totally different and hence irreconcilable logics, neither one of which is as absolute or inclusive.

In their anthology *The Medium and the Light*, Eric McLuhan and Jacek Szklarek have compiled McLuhan's probes into the nature of conversion, the church, religion, and the "god-making machines" of the modern world. They describe his religious reflections as "a golden thread" lining his public pronouncements on the media and social change.

McLuhan argues that *the real message of the church* is in the side effects of the incarnation, that is to say, in Christ's penetration into all of human existence. For him, the ultimate question is, Where do we stand in relation to this reality? Most people prefer to avoid the question. They concern themselves with the content of Christianity, not with its *message* that consists of "being plugged into a person."[13]

When Christian apologists concentrate on the content of the faith, McLuhan contends, they seldom go beyond its efficient cause. But it is in the formal cause that Christianity's real significance lies, that is, where *the manner of Christian being* is communicated. Christian doctrine is only half of the faith—and not the part that operates most powerfully in our lives. Ideally, McLuhan tells us, these two aspects of Christianity should be united, for it is only at the level of a lived Christianity that the medium really *is* the message.[14]

When asked if he thought that the American Catholic church had become too accommodating to the needs of its lay members, McLuhan replied:

> I never came into the Church as a person who was being taught. I came in on my knees. That is *the only* way in. When people start praying, they need truths; that's all. You don't come into the Church by ideas and concepts, and you cannot leave by mere disagreement. It has to be a loss of faith, a loss of participation. You can tell when people leave the Church: they have quit praying. Actively relating to the Church's prayer and sacraments is not done through ideas. Any Catholic today who has an intellectual disagreement with the Church has an illusion. You cannot have an intellectual disagreement with the Church: that's meaningless. The Church is not an intellectual institution. It is a superhuman institution.[15]

For McLuhan, the more pressing theological question for our time was what to do with the Greco-Roman tradition now that it has become the shell and not the content of the faith. Was the Greco-Roman enterprise simply "a political bastion that we can now let sink under the electric waves that now cover the planet? How much of the Greco-Roman mind-set does

---

13. McLuhan, *The Medium and the Light: Reflections of Religion*, ed. Eric McLuhan and Jacek Szlarek (Toronto: Stoddart, 1999), 55.

14. Ibid., 55–56.

15. Marshall McLuhan, "Futurechurch: Edward Waken Interviews Marshall McLuhan," *US Catholic* 42, no. 1 (Jan. 1977): 6–11.

the Church really need to transmit to persons and societies? Can its forms of visual experience and expression be dropped for acoustic and electric man? Can the Church now be introduced directly into the lives of all Africans, of all Orientals, by abandoning itself without question to electric mentality?"[16]

When asked if he wasn't frightened by the implications of his own questions and theories, McLuhan admitted:

> My formation is owing entirely to the left cerebral hemisphere, which is literary. All my values, of course, were nurtured by Greco-Roman civilization. You can easily guess, then, what I am feeling. In a certain way, I also think that this could be the time of the Antichrist. When electricity allows for the simultaneity of all information for every human being, it is Lucifer's moment. He is the greatest electrical engineer. Technically speaking, the age in which we live is certainly favorable to an Antichrist. Just think: each person can instantly be tuned to a "new Christ" and mistake him for the real Christ. At such times it becomes crucial to hear properly and to tune yourself in to the right frequency.[17]

McLuhan hoped that if he could discover the principle of creativity in morals, he would have the master key to future intercultural associations. Faced with information overload, he argued, we had no alternative but to rely upon pattern recognition.

> We must substitute an interest in the media for the previous interest in subjects. This is the logical answer to the fact that the media have substituted themselves for the older world. Even if we should wish to recover that older world, we can do it only by an intensive study of the way in which the media have swallowed it. And no matter how many walls have fallen, the citadel of individual consciousness has not fallen nor is it likely to fall. For it is not accessible to the mass media.[18]

16. McLuhan, *Medium and the Light*, 208–9.
17. Ibid.
18. McLuhan, *Counter Blast*, 132–35.

Here we can see that McLuhan wanted to do for the consumers of modern media what Northrop Frye attempted to do for the readers of literature: make them the heroes of their own quest for meaning and take them to the contemplative center of the mind where the word would become the Word, and the medium the message.

In fact, his slogan "the medium is the message" is just another way of saying "the Word become flesh." For McLuhan, divinity and humanity had become one in Christ, as did form and content, the temporal and the eternal. From McLuhan's perspective, Frye's *Anatomy* was inherently incomplete because the literary center of the modern world had been ingested by the new electronic media. Rhetoric, irony, and myth were no longer aesthetic absolutes, but chased each other around the perimeters of the new sensorium via radio shows and television programs.

Regardless of whether or not McLuhan is right about Gutenberg's movable type causing the shift into modern consciousness, there is no doubt that some kind of transformation has occurred in the way moderns process information and understand culture. His hyperbolic explanations write this transformation up large for all of us to see, and if he is wrong in a few of the particulars or overstates his case, it is a small matter compared to the very big truth he has been able to communicate: we are very different from the ancients.

Less a scholar of communications and more a historian of consciousness, McLuhan made the interior drama of our age more intelligible—providing a view on the clash of cultures and generations taking place within the larger clash of civilizations, exposing the civil wars unfolding between generations and clashing sensoriums. This is where the real battle for the future is shaping up: in the phenomenological wars within civilizations that, if not properly negotiated, could lead to wars between them.

If the old epistemology turns out to be groundless, and the still older eschatology the only useful alternative, then a vision of the end times becomes the place where thought begins. McLuhan took us part of the way there with his refusal to play the old linear, foundationalist game. But perhaps there is less to the new electronic culture than he imagined, and so like many other millennialists, he may have mistook the end of his age for the coming of the Messiah.

McLuhan's media apocalypse, however, still has much to teach us, for he looked squarely into the abyss of our age and, armed with faith, did not flinch until he could describe with precision its cold, lunar landscape. He was, perhaps, the greatest of our modernist critics, because he saw through the works of Joyce and Eliot to their deep structure and philosophical meaning, converting them into elements of his own work—not merely describing them as cultural artifacts situated in space and time.

McLuhan was a Nietzschean culture hero of the joyful wisdom, and it is telling that his Christian faith made this possible, lifting him above and beyond the mesmerizing political harangues and ideological confusions of his day to see the big picture—moving up and down the ladder of Being in an attempt to bring some clarity to our modern confusion of realms. It was an ancient tactic: medieval, Christian, Catholic. But it gave birth to a startling array of insights into our postmodern lives.

Northrop Frye: The Return of "Reverse Causation"

My Christian position is that of Blake reinforced by Emily Dickinson.

Northrop Frye[19]

A serious human life, no matter what religion is invoked, can hardly begin until we see an element of illusion in what is really there, and something real in fantasies about what might be there instead.

Northrop Frye, *The Great Code*[20]

The world counsels us to be silent in evil times, to make use of our reason to defend its own terror and cruelty, to study the great disciplines of art and

19. Northrop Frye, Notebooks 11h, 13: RF 12. Frye's archives are housed in the Pratt Library of Victoria University in Canada.

20. Northrop Frye, *The Great Code: The Bible and Literature* (New York: Harcourt Brace, 1982), 50.

science for the sake of our own aggressions, our desire not to be our brother's
keeper. For the world is terrified of silence and study: it knows that in the calm
mind thy presence appears: it runs from thee shrieking with all its legions
of devils. But we know that thy light cannot be concealed, that thy presence
is not in the thunder and lightning and fire but in the small and still voice
of truth, of peace, and of wisdom. Sanctify our talents that our minds may
re-echo thy praise which resounds from the beauty of nature and the great
works of love and intellect.

Northrop Frye[21]

Northrop Frye was an ordained minister in the United Church of Canada, orthodox in his Christian faith but avant-garde in his systematization
of modern aesthetics into a grand contemplative ordering of the human
imagination: extending the impersonal universalism of Eliot to include all
of Western literature. Taking his lead from Blake, he hypothesized that at
the heart of all literary activity was the quest for identity and extended that
idea through Spengler into an encyclopedic vision of the phantasmagoria
of human history. His later work on the Bible united his Christocentric
worldview with his conception of art as essentially apocalyptic and criticism as allegory. He believed that the Bible contained within it the most
significant modes and genres of fiction, anticipating, and indeed shaping,
the works of all our greatest literary masters—Chaucer, Milton, Blake,
Eliot, and Joyce—but going beyond them in its overt advocacy of a life of
counterhistorical, supraliterary contemplation. For Frye, the ideal reader
of both the Bible and literature takes a journey to the center of the mind
to discover that it doesn't really exist.

His great contribution to contemporary thought was to systematize
Western poetics into a single, all-encompassing contemplative ordering of the human imagination. He hypothesized that at the heart of all
cultural activity lies a revolt of the finite against the indefinite. Our
lives begin and end, but time is eternal. Therefore, we use signs, im-

21. Northrop Frye, *Northrop Frye on Religion*, ed. Alvin A. Lee and Jean O'Grady (Toronto:
University of Toronto Press, 2000), 381.

ages, gestures, words, and myths to describe alternating moments in time. These forms give us light and darkness, summer and winter, and all our other rhythms and contrasts.

Picking up on themes in Genesis, Frye postulates a time before myth, when life had not divided itself from nature and myth was not yet "myth." After the fall the God story could be taken only on faith or ironically. Hence the two poles of the cultural imagination: tragic transcendence and comic immanence.

Once a myth is seen as a story, consciousness is no longer experienced as one with nature; so the individual must embark on a quest for identity, since the identity that comes with one's social and cultural milieu is inherently unconvincing and false. Frye puts it this way:

> In every age there is a structure of ideas, images, beliefs, assumptions, anxieties, and hopes which express the view of man's situation and destiny generally held at that time. I call this structure a mythology, and its units myths. A myth, in this sense, is an expression of man's concern about himself, about his place in the scheme of things, about his relation to society and God, about the ultimate origins and ultimate fate, either of himself or of the human species generally. A mythology is thus a product of human concern, of our involvement with ourselves, and it always looks at the world from a man-centered point of view. The early and primitive myths were stories, mainly stories about gods, and their units were physical images. In more highly structured societies they develop in two different but related directions. In the first place, they develop into literature as we know it, first into folktales and legends of heroes, thence into the conventional plots of fictions and metaphors of poetry. In the second place, they become conceptualized, and become the informing principles of historical and philosophical thought, as the myth of the fall becomes the informing idea of Gibbon's history of Rome, or the myth of the sleeping beauty Rousseau's buried society of nature and reason.[22]

22. Northrop Frye, *The Modern Century: The Whidden Lectures* (Toronto: Oxford University Press, 1967), 105–6.

Hence, mythological thinking is never overcome by science, history, philosophy or theology, but merely transformed into larger unconscious principles. Thus for Frye, we are all on a journey out from under our own personal lives into the transpersonal order of the universally symbolic. This is a journey fraught with the psychological dangers of projection, fusion, and all manner of anxieties of influence. But if these problems can be navigated honestly, a freer self emerges from the narrow identifications of race, culture, and class, and mystical participation with all humanity. The "ideal reader" is at the center of an "intertextual universe," at the still center of the "order of words" where we comprehend the whole and know ourselves to be both the creator and container of our mythologized world. When this happens, we transcend words and apprehend the Word.

Frye sees the ideal reader as dying to the letter of the text (literal reading) and being reborn into its spirit (mythic reading). "A serious human life," Frye tells us, "no matter what religion is invoked, can hardly begin until we see an element of illusion in what is really there, and something real in fantasies about what might be there instead."[23] "In the double vision of a spiritual and a physical world simultaneously present, every moment we have lived through we have also died out of into another order. Our life in resurrection, then, is already here, and waiting to be recognized."[24]

In an eloquent passage, Frye sums up the relationship of literature to religion:

> For the last fifty years I have been studying literature, where the organizing principles are myth, that is, story or narrative, and metaphor, that is, figured language. Here we are in a completely liberal world, the world of the free movement of the spirit. If we read a story there is no pressure to believe in it or act upon it; if we encounter metaphors in poetry, we need not worry about their factual absurdity. Literature incorporates our ideological concerns, but it devotes itself mainly to the primary ones, in both physical and spiritual forms: its fictions show

23. Frye, *Great Code*, 50.
24. Frye, *Northrop Frye on Religion*, 235.

human beings in the primary throes of surviving, loving, prospering, and fighting with the frustrations that block these things. It is at once a world of relaxation, where even the most terrible tragedies are still called plays, and a world of far greater intensity than ordinary life affords. It does, in short, everything that can be done for people except transform them. It creates a world that the spirit can live in, but it does not make us spiritual beings. It would be absurd to see the New Testament as only a work of literature: it is all the more important, therefore, to realize that it is written in the language of literature, the language of myth and metaphor. The Gospels give us the life of Jesus in the form of myth: what they say is, "This is what happens when the Messiah comes to the world." One thing that happens when the Messiah comes to the world is that he is despised and rejected, and searching in the nooks and crannies of the Gospel text for a credibly historical Jesus is merely one more excuse for despising and rejecting him. Myth is neither historical nor anti-historical: it is counter-historical. Jesus is not presented as a historical figure, but as a figure who drops into history from another dimension of reality, and thereby shows what the limitations of the historical perspective are.[25]

To save modern humanity from its hubristic, reductive, pseudo-scientific self-descriptions, we must recover the myths that inform our lives, not pretend to have transcended them into some "higher" literal state of consciousness that is itself the expression of an unconscious mythology. Thus, the center of the literary universe is whatever work we happen to be reading at the time, just as God is present in whatever person we happen to be with.

"Human beings live in a constructed envelope called culture or civilization," Frye reminds us. "What is genuinely creative disturbs our settled reality, recovering our repressed social past and *redemptively envisioning an ideal society* in a totally humanized nature. Literary critics do not judge the writer, except incidentally: they work with the writer in judging the human condition."[26] What separates the Bible from literary myth is its call

25. Ibid., 178.
26. Ibid., 196. Italics mine.

to an active faith, which is "a continuous sequence of committed actions guided by a vision."[27]

In *The Great Code,* Frye writes:

> What typology really is as a mode of thought, what it both assumes and leads to, is a theory of history, or more accurately of historical process: an assumption that there is some meaning and point to history, and that sooner or later some event or events will occur which will indicate what that meaning or point is, and so become the anti-type of what has happened previously.[28]

So when a literary trope is repeated or a myth replayed, it is not a simple recapitulation, but a recreation that can redeem and reawaken experience itself. *Literary archetypes function as instances of "reverse causation," refurbishing experience with new meaning and significance.* Literature and language constantly renew the earth, recapitulating in constantly new minidramas the unfolding of the ontological vibrancy of human experience. Karl Marx once famously remarked that history always repeats itself: "The first time as tragedy, the second time as farce." Frye would only add "and the third time as romance, the fourth time as comedy, the fifth time as tragedy again, and so on ad infinitum in a repetitive cycle until the end of time." Art is recycled revelation.

The church, Frye argues, must stop obstinately opposing literature to science and instead "present its faith as the emancipation and the fulfillment of reason."[29] By firmly separating Gospel from law, the church can mediate between them. That is to say, by identifying the Gospels as an expression of the myth of freedom, Frye disconnects Christianity from the powers that be, and like Blake, reconnects it to the sovereignty of the human imagination.

Frye saw sectarian ideologies as the death of culture. The Bible can overcome ideology when seen as a source of meta-mythological reflection that

27. Ibid., 356.
28. Frye, *Great Code*, 80–81.
29. Ibid., 267.

points the reader to the contemplative center of any and all symbolic structures. In the New Testament, the Old Testament mythology is turned into
literature: rejected *and* affirmed, both "seen through" *and* "fulfilled," exposed
as fictive and yet acknowledged as anagogical. Modern secular thought
is uncomfortable with such apocalyptic double vision. Frye's *Anatomy of
Criticism* is, in this sense, a rendering of the phantasmagoria of the human
imagination for secular minds suffering from an incapacity to grasp the
transcendent meaning of literary figures and for religious minds who need
literature to decalcify the ossified forms inherent in their own doctrines
and dogmas.

And though some critics dismiss Frye as a liberal humanist whose
critical approach was ineffective in overcoming the political injustices
and cultural stagnation of late industrial capitalism, Frye could point to
the equally dismal record of political critics in dislodging the moral com-
placency of the contemporary bourgeois mind.[30] From Frye's perspective,
the theorists themselves need to renew their own critiques through the
anagogical imagination.

For Frye, one of the primary purposes of literary criticism is to separate
the renewing power of myth from the mystifications of ideology. To accomplish this, the critic must translate the unconscious mythology at work
in the text into everyday language, thereby putting literature into its proper
place—not as a vehicle of ideology—but as a medium of human revelation,
the source and substance of all epiphanies, idealizations, and revelatory
insights. Only after we recover our myths, he argues, may we "pass from
state to community, from exploitation to imaginative work, from culture
as a privilege of a few, to culture as the inner condition of everyone."[31]

Culture "tends to create out of actual society an ideal order of liberty,
equality, and fraternity."[32] For Frye, the poet transcends ideology by
attaching the literary work to traditions and conventions and meta-

30. Terry Eagleton, *Literary Theory* (Minneapolis: University of Minnesota Press, 1983), 199.
31. Northrop Frye, *Spiritus Mundi: Essays* (Bloomington: Indiana University Press, 1976),
110.
32. Northrop Frye, *Stubborn Structure* (Ithaca, N.Y.: Cornell University Press, 1970), 254.

phoric structures that go beyond his or her social condition. What frees the artist is the reworking of a universal archetype or image that opens up on an entire cosmos of hitherto "lost" human possibilities. In this sense, literature is not just a passive echo of the social ideal of its time, nor is it completely "embedded" in an unconscious cultural ideology; otherwise, it could never be original, transgenerational, or transcultural.[33]

Frye—like Blake, Dostoyevsky, and Berdyaev (not to mention T. S. Eliot and James Joyce)—sees the Bible as the formulation and superstructure of the culture in which we are embedded: a culture that they worked to renew, setting its mythology against its ideology in an attempt to desacralize existing secular institutions and render holy a saving remnant of apocalyptic hope.

This is why Frye believed that the study of "anagoges"—a term he later replaced with "archetypal repetition"—would provide "the missing piece of contemporary thought which, once supplied, would unite the whole pattern of contemporary existence."[34] That is to say, once we see through the hubris of our own literal imaginations to the universal archetypal structures underneath, their power over us as structures will disappear, and we will find ourselves at the center of a contemplative vision of history free from the idolatries and unconscious heresies of our age.

Jacques Ellul: Power Politics, Technology, and the Media

The word of God can be proclaimed only by someone who places himself outside "the world," while staying at the very heart of the questioning that goes on within it.

Jacques Ellul, *Living Faith*[35]

33. Frye, *Great Code*, 108.

34. Northrop Frye, *Fearful Symmetry: A Study of William Blake* (Princeton, N.J.: Princeton University Press, 1948), 424, 425.

35. Jacques Ellul, *Living Faith* (New York: Harper & Row, 1980), 276, 277.

Jacques Ellul is an orthodox Protestant who has written critiques of technology, modern politics, and the mass media, as well as books on prayer and anarchism. His book exposing the intellectual commonplaces of contemporary culture is at once an avant-garde exposé of the technocratic herd mentality of the new bourgeoisie and at the same time a defense of traditional Christian virtues. Ivan Illich once commented upon his influence:

> Some of us have read him [Ellul] as a great commentator on the Bible, others, as a philosopher of technology. But few have seen him as the man who simultaneously challenges the reflection of both the philosopher and the believer. He reminds the philosopher of technology, who studies patent, observable phenomena, to be aware of the possibility that his subject may be too terrible to be grasped by reason alone. And he leads the believer to deepen his Biblical faith and eschatological hope in the face of two uncomfortable and disturbing truths . . . [that of] modern technique and its malevolent consequences [and that of the] subversion of the Gospel—its transformation into an ideology called Christianity.[36]

Ellul, like other Christian macrohistorians, sees modern society as dominated by the pursuit of economic and technological efficiency that has led to the transformation of virtually every human practice and institution. World War I, World War II, Hiroshima, and the rise of totalitarian ideologies and regimes are all manifestations of this focus upon efficiency and control to the exclusion of virtually every other value. The manufacture of products and services have become more important than "civic life," and the entertainment industry—once seen as a frivolous pursuit of distraction—has actually eclipsed high culture as the source of socialization and political formation.

Yet the morally debilitating effects of these changes have been masked by blaming the ensuing social problems on outsiders, pariahs, and fiends. How else can one explain the widespread indifference to the massive inequalities of wealth in the world or the continuing existence of curable poverty and economic misery? How else can we understand the increasing narcissism

36. Ivan Illich, "An Address to 'Master Jacques,'" *Ellul Forum* 13 (July 1994): 16.

and self-absorption of those living in the most economically successful societies in human history?

In the author's forward to the revised American edition of *The Technological Society,* Elull described his own relationship to contemporary culture:

> I do not limit myself to describing my feelings with cold objectivity in the manner of a research worker reporting what he sees under a microscope. I am keenly aware that I am myself involved in technological civilization, and that its history is also my own. I may be compared rather with a physician or physicist who is describing a group situation in which he is himself involved. The physician in an epidemic, the physicist exposed to radioactivity: in such situations the mind may remain cold and lucid, and the method objective, but there is inevitably a profound tension of the whole being.[37]

Ellul became a Marxist at age nineteen, and a Christian at twenty-two.[38] His religious faith evolved out of the Death of God movement and the response of the neo-orthodox theologians Bultmann, Barth, Niebuhr, and Tillich. According to Darrel Fasching, the Barthian dialectic, in which the Gospels both judge and renew the world, helped to shape Ellul's theological perspective.[39] For Ellul, "that which desacralizes a given reality, itself in turn becomes the new sacred reality."[40] He applied this reading of the Scriptures to the emerging technological society—defining technique as "the totality of methods rationally arrived at and having absolute efficiency (for a given stage of development) in every field of human activity"[41] and then setting the biblical revelation of man in opposition to it.

For Ellul, technique is not just the society of machines but the entire society of efficient techniques.[42] In other words, modern technology is a

---

37. Jacques Ellul, *The Technological Society,* trans. John Wilkinson (New York: Knopf, 1964), xvii–xviii.

38. Darrel J. Fasching, *The Thought of Jacques Ellul: A Systematic Exposition* (New York: E. Mellen Press, 1981), 2.

39. Ibid., 7.

40. Ibid., 35.

41. Ibid., xxv.

42. Ibid., 15.

total phenomenon of the entire civilization, the defining force of a new social order in which efficiency is not just an option but a necessity imposed upon every human activity.[43] Propaganda seduces people into consenting to this; the mass media are the tools of propaganda—creating the illusion that people are free and creative when in fact they are mind-numbingly conformed to the principle of "efficient ordering."[44]

Ellul's seminal work, *The Technological Society* (1964), was originally titled *La Technique: l'enjen du siècle*, "the stake of the century." In it, he argues that the rationality of technique creates an artificial system that "eliminates or subordinates the natural world."[45] Simulations have replaced nature, policy has replaced social theory, public administration has replaced policy, and demographics rule public administration, with the consequence that education is reduced to schooling, news to broadcasting, books to publishing, sports to spectacle, and "persons" to therapeutic problems.

The technological society has, in other words, changed the entire environment we live in, yet we still haven't admitted that we are not the masters of our tools and techniques, that they rule us, or that our institutions shape our thinking. We "feel" free because we remain oblivious to the technologically "bound" nature of our own existence. We have all become ghosts in an autonomous socioeconomic machine, ashamed of our own private subjectivity, or rather, burdened by it, knowing that our one-of-a-kind inner lives are embarrassingly unnecessary to the great collective endeavors of our time. Jean Baudrillard, in his book *Forget Foucault,* describes these developments:

> Nowadays one no longer says: "You've got a soul and you must save it," but: "You've got a sexual nature, and you must find out how to use it well." "You've got an unconscious, and you must learn how to liberate it." "You've got a body, and you must know how to enjoy it." "You've got a libido, and you must know how to spend it."[46]

43. Ibid., 17.
44. Ibid., 18.
45. Ibid., 17.
46. Jean Baudrillard, *Forget Foucault* (New York: Semiotexte, 1987), 24.

Ellul blames our inability to extricate ourselves from this situation, in part, on the way we use words and fall prey to artificial images:

> This, then, is our situation today: through the eruption of unlimited artificial images, we have reduced truth to the order of reality and banished the shy and *fleeting* expression of truth. . . . No longer are we surrounded by fields, woods, and rivers, but by signs, signals, billboards, screens, labels, and trademarks: this is our universe. And when the screen shows us a living reality, such as people's faces or other countries, this is still a fiction: it is a constructed and recombined reality.[47]

This process is identical to that of idolatry in the earliest times, but its objects are different because the earlier "idols" no longer exist. We no longer make an image of a powerful bull to symbolize fertility: instead we use the image to "advertise" various machines and electricity. Just as the king once had magical powers, now movie stars and dictators have it. Propaganda gives us symbolic persons, such as "Youth Personified," or "The Terrorist," and even "Woman" is given back her role as idol through media images.[48] Hence, Camille Paglia links popular culture to pornography and paganism.[49]

But unlike Paglia and the worshipful fans of Madonna, Marilyn Monroe, and Elvis Presley, Ellul does not see the rise of the mass media as a liberating return of the repressed. For him, like McLuhan, it is a form of mesmerism that can only be broken by listening to God. Not surprisingly, Ellul has emphasized prayer as a way to see through the fog of culture. So while the culture critics seek the meaning of our times in the depths of its prehistory, Ellul turns instead to the end times and revelation.

> God makes it plain that law is not justice (the justice that God himself establishes as such), that human peace is not peace, that human virtue is not the blessing that God alone can say, that the human community is not com-

---

47. Jacques Ellul, *The Humiliation of the Word*, trans. Joyce Main Hanks (Grand Rapids: Eerdmans, 1985), 228.

48. Ibid., 229.

49. See Camille Paglia, *Vamps and Tramps* (New York: Vintage Press, 1994), 260.

munion with God, that human love is not Love. In other words, religion and revelation cover the same territory, though while religion sacralizes and absolutizes human realities, revelation desacralizes and relativizes them—the latter of which is extremely useful as far as humans are concerned. And yet we might well feel like saying: "But why doesn't this God let us work things out all by ourselves? Why not let us organize our little societies and blunder through in this world, a job we handle fairly well? Why does this God come to disturb us and cause confusion?" The reason is, precisely for humanity's sake, so that people can't take themselves for God, with all the consequences we have seen deriving from that. If the nation is not a religious value, any more than law or science, if one lives in a relative world where everything is constantly being relativized, then peace is infinitely easier, as are compromise and reconciliation. But you can't relativize things except vis-à-vis an absolute, and this is a self-revealing absolute. What an admirable decision on God's part: he does not reveal himself as a religious absolute, but as love, as powerlessness, as one who comes down to our level and thus devalues everything else.[50]

By using sociological categories, Jacques Ellul exposes the idols of efficiency and control. Without lapsing into ideological critiques or sweeping denunciations, his nuanced assessment of modern life—tragic, Christian, and yet still ethically and economically progressive—makes possible a measured prophetic witness from within the belly of our postmodern sociohistorical "beast."

The key to his analysis lies in his critique of the "sacralizing of the secular"—the worship of method and technique as the answer to all the world's problems. This belief in scientific progress as the agent of social salvation has the paradoxical effect of making us all less free at the very moment we become more powerful. This loss of freedom is covered up by propaganda that sells the idea of a utopian future brought about by obedience to the new "necessities" of efficiency, command, and control.

50. Ellul, *Living Faith*, 143–44.

Television and radio are compelling because they concentrate our attention on a particular sensory experience, disconnecting the other senses and
thereby also the intellect from effective sensory processing. A suspension of
disbelief takes place unconsciously. We know we aren't watching reality, but
the fact that we *think* we have already factored that fact into our experience
predisposes us to accept what we see as true. The medium is the message
always already accepted by the person distracted by the so-called content of
the program and by his own misperceiving "critical consciousness." Hence,
the alienation is complete, the audience's subjection reinforced, and the
media's power confirmed at precisely the moment one criticizes its "content."
Marshall McLuhan wrote: "All the new media, including the press, are art
forms which have the power of imposing, like poetry, their own assumptions.
The new media are not ways of relating us to the old 'real' world: they are
the real world and they reshape what remains of the old world at will."[51]

In order to overcome this moral/intellectual enslavement, Ellul recom-
mends a proactive, critical effort to desacralize modern institutions. This can
be accomplished only by (1) a thorough sociological analysis of the powers
that be, exposing their hidden idolatries and false absolutes, thereby opening
up zones of freedom within the power structure where human relationships
and free expression can flourish and (2) deepening our appreciation, understanding, and devotion to God and to humanity. In this sense, the Christian
must judge and renew the world—see it as it actually is and yet continue
to "actualize the eschaton" whatever the current situation. By "actualizing
the eschaton" Ellul simply means bringing the apocalyptic witness of the
liberated Christ to bear on the present muddled realities of life.

In 1966 Ellul published *A Critique of the New Commonplaces*, a book
that exposes the prejudices of the modern. The popular bromide: "We must
follow the current of history," he argues, should be replaced by the critical
insight that the world progresses only from the thoughts of those who op-
pose it. "The main thing is to be sincere with yourself" should be replaced
by the notion of how hard it is to be sincere. And the idea that "the people

51. McLuhan, *Counter Blast*, 52.

have come of age" recognized as a grandiose conceit contradicted by the front page of virtually any newspaper in the world.

And there are others: the truism that "women find their freedom and dignity in work," he argues, ensures that the culture will make every effort to get both sexes into the workplace. Moreover, the notion that "the spiritual side of life cannot develop until the standard of living is raised," a notion re-inforced by business-school bastardizations of Abraham Maslow's "hierarchy of needs," serves as yet another justification for bourgeois materialism when it has been pretty much established that spiritual greatness often blossoms under the most abject of economic circumstances.

Now some of these new commonplaces aren't as popular as they once were, and some have been replaced by more obnoxious inanities, such as "Appearances *are* reality" and "It's the economy, stupid." But what is worth noting here is the rhetorical method Elull employs to carve out a small zone for original thought. Like Flaubert, who wrote a satirical dictionary of commonplace ideas, Elull recognizes that we must first demolish the omnipresent untruths that clutter our minds before we can begin to search for alternatives. Milan Kundera called this cluttered intellectual environ-ment "the non-thought of received ideas" and saw it as the defining feature of "the modernization of stupidity."[52]

Ellul's opposition to the non-thought of received ideas can be traced back to his work with the French Resistance during the Second World War, and his defense of those accused of treason by the French government after the war. This shift in roles is characteristic of Ellul's skepticism toward human institutions: he sides instinctively with the outsiders, the oppressed, the vic-timized, and the accused—and yet nevertheless continues to engage in the all-too-human pursuit of justice in a world prone to political compromise and amoral expediencies. In his book *The New Demons*, Ellul wrote:

> It is not technology itself which enslaves us, but the transfer of the sacred into technology. That is what keeps us from exercising the critical faculty, and

52. Milan Kundera, *The Art of the Novel* (New York: Grove Press, 1988), 162–63.

from making technology serve human development. It is not the state which enslaves us, not even a centralized police state. It is the sacral transfiguration . . . which makes us direct our worship to this conglomerate of offices. . . . The religious, which man in our situation is bound to produce, is the surest agent of his alienation, of his acceptance of the powers which enslave him.[53]

Thus Ellul's politics is not ordered by any Machiavellian calculations, but by constant reference to the ultimate end of things, the apocalyptic triumph of good over evil. The very existence of the state is premised on the existence of chaos; the state is the human counter-chaos sustained by propaganda in order to appear as natural and just. Both the state and the media thus deny God. And yet Ellul insists that the end is already present in the world. "It is here already as a secret force, both evoking and also provoking our means. We have to be obedient to the end, not as a goal to be reached and which we may possess, but also and at the same time as a given fact, something already there, a presence which is active too. Hope then is an actual reality which makes ultimacy present and active. Hope actualizes the last days, the *eschaton*."[54]

Therefore, Christians are called to liberate the city from its own over-whelming ambitions by living on apocalyptic hope. By doing this, they become God's means for inserting freedom into the existing political order. Darrell J. Fasching in his brilliant synopsis of Ellul's ideas put it this way:

Clearly then, for Ellul the Christian vocation is a call to incarnate the freedom of God, for the purpose of opening up and sustaining the eschatological direction of creation and history. But today, he observes, Christians largely conform to the sacral values of the technological society. They have forfeited their birthright of freedom for a pot of soup; for security, progress, and happiness in the technological world of abundance. How then can they assume

---

53. Jacques Ellul, *The New Demons* (New York: Seabury Press, 1975), 206–7.
54. Jacques Ellul, *The Politics of God and the Politics of Man* (Grand Rapids: Eerdmans, 1972), 136, quoted in Fasching, *Thought of Jacques Ellul*, 95–96.

their revolutionary vocation of freedom? For Ellul the answer is—through apocalyptic hope.[55]

It is this hope that allows us to give witness to God's kingdom in an uncomprehending world, a world that thinks it has already absorbed faith, Scripture, even church and prayer, into its worldly, utilitarian agenda. Again Ellul says it far more eloquently than I can when he remarks:

> The efficacy we seek can only be that of a radical alteration of the world and society. It is the efficacy of event as opposed to institution, of tension against the accepted line, of nonconformity. In sum, it is an efficacy which stands opposed to that of the world. Yet it is no less real. It is the efficacy which shatters unanimity, the efficacy of heretics and sectarians. Nor is this negative, for the positive simply cannot exist without it.[56]

I once taught a class with the president of our university on the role of higher education in the contemporary world. It was a spirited discussion class with many guest speakers and students from every discipline. One of our guests had designed a virtual reality computer program that allowed architects to "walk through" buildings they had designed in their heads—an innovation greeted as a great breakthrough for designers—especially for a handicapped designer who had difficulty walking around structures.

I asked our guest whether his innovation gave architects more freedom or less? Might it not be better *not* to walk through a simulation of one's own design but to create it completely in the realm of pure imaginative possibility unfettered by any practical considerations or simulated forms? He took my question as an insult. By questioning the absolute good of his achievement, I had committed a secular heresy. And when I foolhardily continued by asking if he had considered *any* downside to his innovation, he couldn't even fathom my question.

55. Fasching, *Thought of Jacques Ellul*, 81.
56. Ellul, *Politics of God*, 141.

I was dealing here with a technological true believer anointed by professionalism and consecrated by the gods of progress. It was a wonder I
wasn't burned at the stake! But if Ellul is right, we must treat all technological accomplishments, even those of genius, with a grain of salt. Nothing
constitutes an absolute gain on reality; nothing frees us completely from
our conditioned state; and anything that claims it does is more myth than
reality. Apply this contrarian thinking to the current commonplaces of
contemporary politics, culture, economics, and the media, and you have
Ellul's prophetic response to contemporary society, a response tailor-made
for intellectual martyrdom.

Ivan Illich: In the Mirror of the Past

> Yes, I know, I know very well, that it is madness to seek to turn the waters
> of the river back to their source, and that it is only the ignorant who seek to
> find in the past a remedy for their present ills; but I know too that everyone
> who fights for any ideal whatever, although his ideal may seem to lie in the
> past, is driving the world on to the future, and that the only reactionaries are
> those who find themselves at home in the present. Every supposed restora-
> tion of the past is a creation of the future, and if the past which it is sought
> to restore is a dream, something imperfectly known, so much the better.
> The march, as ever, is towards the future, and he who marches is getting
> there, even though he march walking backwards. And who knows if that is
> not the better way!
>
> Miguel de Unamuno, *Tragic Sense of Life*[57]

The idea that by not responding to [someone] when [they] call upon my fidelity, I thereby personally offend God is fundamental to [my] understanding
[of] what Christianity is about. And the mystery which I am interested in
contemplating [is] the consequences of the perversion of faith throughout

---

57. Miguel de Unamuno, *Tragic Sense of Life,* trans. J. E. Crawford Flitch (New York: Dover
Publications, 1954), 321.

history which haunts us at the end of the 20th century [that] is exactly related to my understanding of [this] sin.

Ivan Illich, *The Corruption of Christianity*[58]

As an ordained Catholic priest working with the poor, Ivan Illich approached contemporary social problems from a theological perspective, and although his preferential option for the poor was hardly avant-garde, his countercultural views as to exactly how that option should be exercised were radically plebeian and antimodernist. He believed that the Enlightenment project to accomplish moral ends with amoral tools had clearly failed and that the institutions embodying those projects no longer deserved our allegiance. The way forward was backward, back to the original virtues that predated modernity and shaped and defined classical civilization.

In 1968 Ivan Illich was called by the Vatican to appear before the Congregation for the Doctrine of the Faith. As the director of the Center for Intercultural Documentation in Cuernevaca, he had publicly protested the "The Papal Volunteers," a Catholic version of the Peace Corps, because he saw them as part of the global assault against subsistence farming. He warned that building schools, hospitals, and highways in poor agrarian countries could produce greater social polarization between the classes, and new forms of poverty and alienation, and would make local economies dependent on global markets and therefore prone to military "solutions" that would ruin their ecologies and ultimately destroy whatever remained of their indigenous cultures.

Although Illich insisted that his views were entirely orthodox and within the teachings of the church, he withdrew from the priesthood a year later. He continued to write about the effects of development and argued that contemporary culture, including Christianity itself, was being corrupted by the professionalization of virtue. The ethos of professionalism within the emerging global service economy was having the paradoxical effect of transforming the spiritual injunction to love one's neighbor into a collective

58. Ivan Illich, *The Corruption of Christianity* (Montreal: Canadian Broadcast Corporation, 2000), 9.

attempt to systematically eliminate risk and contingency from human affairs. He wrote:

> Part of the genius of modern institutions is that they developed rituals that speak to every aspect of people's desires: to vanity, to the love of beauty, to the pursuit of truth and order, to all sensual delight and, coming full circle to the origins of humans—according to scientific literature—they especially speak to fear.[59]

These new rituals constituted, for Illich, a form of soul theft that replaced moral growth with dispiriting rules and procedures—putting power in the hands of those least qualified to wield it and taking it away from the very people the system was meant to serve. Only by de-schooling society and de-professionalizing the professions could authentically moral values born of risk and sacrifice make their way back into our unjust, ingeniously self-promoting body politic, where international social workers helped the poor by making sure local ranchers could buy their property and then retrain them for jobs in the computer industry.

Illich forced both the left and the right to question the effects their own professional privileges were having upon the quality of their thought. Clearly, Enlightenment rationalism had not produced the promised utopias: human perversity and violence were proving to be far more intractable beasts than anyone had imagined. But Illich carried his analysis even further back into history than either McLuhan or Ellul, back to the somatic transformations of felt existence in the age of agriculture, examining how our words have changed and how our remade consciences allow us to endure the suffering and poverty of so many people.

In his book with Barry Sanders, *ABC: The Alphabetization of the Popular Mind,* Illich traces the etymology of key words back to their medieval and classical usages in order to make clear exactly how the educational system and mass media have altered their meanings and how the popular mind has fallen under the influence of whole new argots

---

59. Ivan Illich, *Tools for Conviviality* (New York: Harper & Row, 1973), 5.

such as "Newspeak" and "Uniquack." These jargons fill the language with "amoeba words" that collapse technical terms with social trends in order to generate forms of deception, lies, and falsity—remaking the universe of discourse into one large web of abstractions, nonevents, and simulations of virtue.

Illich believes that many of our current social problems derive from the way language has been transformed from a medium for fresh and original communication into an object to be manipulated. We live in an age of manufactured texts, contrived messages, blocks of discourse, unread downloads, and unreadable metadiscourses. Try to talk to a school administrator about the curriculum or to a politician about legislation without using jargon. It's not possible. And this is why our public schools are failing, our political rhetoric is becoming more and more specious, and the buzz of commerce and hype is drowning out our solitude.

Illich, for example, examines the evolution of the word *energy*, which originally denoted "vigor in speech." In the nineteenth century it was used as a technical term in physics, then adapted to describe nature's more general potential. He remarks:

> For the last hundred years, the term has been used in physics to verbalize an increasingly abstract alternative energy or energy needs. We must be forever conscious of the fact that we do not know what such words mean. We use the words like words from Scripture, like a gift from above. Furthermore, we gratefully transfer the power to define their meanings to an expertocratic hierarchy to which we do not belong. The word "energy" in this context is used neither with common sense, nor with the senseless precision of science, but almost like a sub-linguistic grunt—a nonsense word. Energy, like sexuality, transportation, education, communication, information, crisis, problem, solution, role, and dozens of other words, belongs, in this sense, to the same class.[60]

60. Ivan Illich, *ABC: The Alphabetization of the Popular Mind* (San Francisco: North Point Press, 1988), 106.

These words all breed the same kinds of confusion: a Babel so vast that not even Wittgenstein could show us the way out. And yet, rather than exposing this fraud and resisting it, our best minds and institutions run headlong into it, adopting "Uniquack" and "Newspeak" as their official languages. And it's not just English that has been overrun by these techno-hieroglyphics but also modern Spanish, French, and German. Today's professionals neither affirm nor deny; they give signs, produce ten-pound reports, and speak in code.[61]

In a lecture given in Hanover, Germany, entitled "Health as One's Own Responsibility: No Thank You!" Illich pointed out that the word *responsibility*, like many other moral terms, has come, in our time, to mean the exact opposite of its original meaning. *Responsibility* no longer means "self-limitation" but self-actualization and consumption. To be a "responsible" parent, you must supply all kinds of products and services to your child, just as being *a responsible* consumer means planning your purchases and researching your investments. Being "responsible" for one's health, he argued, now means "the smooth integration of your immune system into a socioeconomic world system" and "the interiorization of global systems into the self, in the manner of a categorical imperative."[62]

These remarks are made all the more poignant by the fact that Illich was suffering from cancer at the time he made them and refusing medical treatment. "Renunciation" had become, for him, both a political and existential statement, and yet, because of his self-sacrifice, he was accused of "irresponsibility"! This drove him to further question the entire modern lexicon. He remarked in an interview toward the end of his life:

> There is no way out of this world. I live in a manufactured reality ever further removed from creation. And I know today what that signifies,

---

61. I once did a little research to find out why the ballot propositions in California were so unreadable. I actually spoke with one of the authors of these propositions, and he told me that he didn't really "write" the proposition himself but simply copied part of the text from a law already on the books in another state, and then combined that with a few other passages sent to him by a lobbyist. (The proposition "passed" overwhelmingly.)

62. Ivan Illich, *Ellul Studies Forum* 8 (Jan. 1992): 4.

what horror threatens each of us. A few decades ago, I did not yet know it. At that time, it seemed possible that I could share responsibility for the re-making of this manufactured world. Today, I finally know what powerlessness is. "Responsibility" is now an illusion. In such a world, "being healthy" is reduced to a combination of techniques, protection of the environment, and adaptation to the consequences of techniques, all three of which are, inevitably, privileges.[63]

"We no longer have a word for courageous, disciplined, self-critical renunciation accomplished in community," he said, "but that is what I am talking about. I will call it *askesis*."[64] By *askesis,* Illich does not mean mortification of the flesh or self-loathing of any kind, but rather an "epistemological discipline" that purges us of those modern concepts that make vices seem like virtues and nonevents seem real.

The power of resignation, as a species of self-abnegation, is beauti-fully described by Karl Polanyi in *The Great Transformation* as one of the great engines of human cultural development.

> Resignation was ever the font of man's strength and new hope. Man accepted the reality of death and built the meaning of his bodily life upon it. He resigned himself to the truth that he had a soul to lose and that there was worse than death, and founded his freedom upon it. He resigns himself, in our time, to the reality of society which means the end of that freedom. But again life springs from ultimate resignation. Uncomplaining acceptance of the reality of society gives man indomi-table courage and strength to remove injustice and unfreedom. As long as he is true to his task of creating more abundant freedom for all, he need not fear that either power or planning will turn against him and destroy the freedom he is building by their instrumentality. This is the meaning of freedom in a complex society: it gives us all the certainty we need.[65]

63. Ibid.
64. Ibid.
65. Karl Polanyi, *The Great Transformation* (Boston: Beacon Press, 1964), 258.

Freedom, in other words, grows out of a resignation to necessity; but in the modern world, this dynamic has reversed itself. "Resignation" is seen as "irresponsibility." We are so committed to the active life that we can no longer even imagine what we have lost in our frenzied efforts to remake the world according to our own desires.

This reading of modern history as the story of the demise of contemplative culture (and the ascetic virtues that came with it) is made a bit clearer by Illich's remarks regarding how the modern media and our educational institutions have taken "the silence out of language." They do this, he tells us, by saying more than can be said and by exploiting the hypnotic power of sensory and information overloads to manipulate and overwhelm. Politicians, advertisers, bureaucrats, and professionals of all kinds pollute our shared social space with their overdetermined "communications" to such a degree that there is no longer any democratic commons or shared solitude in our lives. Illich explains:

> Just as the commons of space are vulnerable and can be destroyed by the motorization of traffic, so the commons of speech are vulnerable and can easily be destroyed by the encroachment of modern means of communication. The issue which I propose for discussion should therefore be clear: how to counter the encroachment of new, electronic devices and systems upon commons that are more subtle and more intimate to our being that either grasslands or roads—commons that are at least as valuable as silence. Silence, according to Western and Eastern tradition alike, is necessary for the emergence of persons. It is taken from us by machines that ape people. We could easily be made increasingly dependent on machines for speaking and for thinking, as we are already dependent on machines for moving. Such a transformation of the environment from a commons to a productive resource constitutes the most fundamental form of environmental degradation.[66]

66. Ivan Illich, "Silence Is a Commons," in *In the Mirror of the Past: Lectures and Address 1978–1990* (New York: Marion Boyars, 1992), 53.

In describing the origins of his infamous claim that we need to "de-school" society, Illich makes it clear that what bothers him is the administration and "the professionalization of learning"—not *learning* per se.

> When . . . I began to engage in a phenomenology of schooling, I first asked myself, What am I studying? Quite definitely, I was not studying what other people told me this was, namely, the most practical arrangement for imparting education, or for creating equality, because I saw that most of the people were stupefied by this procedure, were actually told that they couldn't learn on their own and became disabled and crippled. Secondly, I had the evidence that it promoted a new kind of self-inflicted injustice. So I said to myself, Let me define as schooling the compulsory attendance in groups of no more than fifty and no less than fifteen, of age-specific cohorts of young people around one person called a teacher, who has more schooling than they. And then I asked myself, what kind of a liturgy is used there to generate the belief that this is a social enterprise that has some kind of autonomy from the law? I came to the conclusion that this was a myth-making, a mytho-poetic ritual.[67]

It isn't that schools fail to fulfill their charge to "serve society"; it is that in doing so, they change "learning" into "conforming," providing international corporations and modern industry with literate but docile, uncritical consumers incapable of grasping the oddity of their own peculiar historical moment. Illich attempts to expose this gigantic fraud by providing us with global, transnational historical reevaluations of words, meanings, and institutions.

I am reminded here of Jacques Derrida's recent reflections on "forgiveness."[68] He argues that forgiveness is impossible because it requires forgiving the unforgivable. One can "forgive" only in the more conditional sense of undergoing political and psychological processes of reconciliation. But one must never think that reconciliation is the same thing as forgiveness, for that term, *forgiveness,* must be kept "impossible" if it is to be of any use to us.

67. David Cayley, *Ivan Illich in Conversation* (Ontario: Anasi Press, 1992), 65, 66.
68. See *On Cosmopolitanism and Forgiveness* (New York: Routledge, 2001).

This is the kind of philosophical move Illich makes all the time—rescuing lost words, "impossible" concepts, and misplaced values from modern misrepresentations. No one else so deftly exposes the shifting meanings of "vernacular language," the false modern history of gender roles and race relations, or the miseducation provided by our schools.

Illich's unique method of intellectual inquiry (centered upon week-long brainstorming sessions with like-minded scholars) provides us with a working model for an alternative form of scholarship, giving us an alternative to the university's publish-or-perish system, with its "state philosophers" and "think tanks," ideological hired guns, and tenured reactionaries.

If there is a failing here, it isn't the one he's most often accused of: Ivan Illich is not an extremist. If anything, he doesn't carry his social and political critiques *far enough.* He never systematically dismantles the institutions of the "self," and so, unlike Percy, Merton, or Kerouac, he never teaches us how to "de-self" ourselves in a world of psychological projections. His attention is aimed almost entirely at institutions and social practices.

Like Dorothy Day, Illich suffered for his beliefs, and like her, his work raised almost as many questions as it answered. But perhaps more than any other contemporary Christian social critic, he exposes the easy conscience of our professional classes and makes us think twice about how deeply we are embedded in the self-aggrandizing distortions of our ignoble epoch.

It was left to René Girard, however, to carry this critique of modernity forward as part of a new anthropology, tracing the scapegoat myth back to its origin in the birth of civilization and in the emergence of the interior life.

René Girard: On the End of All World Mythologies

Ordinary heroes who kill their enemies are not really heroes because the people they kill would have died sooner or later; they are actually killing corpses. But someone who is fighting delusions and is able to kill that enemy is a hero in the true sense of the word.

Dalai Lama XIV, *The Way to Freedom*[69]

No one takes the trouble to reflect uncompromisingly about the enigma of a historical situation that is without precedent: the death of all cultures.

René Girard, *Things Hidden since the Foundation of the World*[70]

René Girard began as an avant-garde literary critic who disclosed the psychological dynamics of mimetic desire in modernist fiction. "Mimetic desire" is the notion that human beings have a basic feeling of existential lack that leads them to look to a model who seems to possess a greater fullness of being. The desires of the model are imitated in the hope of acquiring a similar fullness of being.

Girard remarks:

When modern theorists envisage man as a being who knows what he wants, or who at least possesses an "unconscious" that knows for him, they may simply have failed to perceive the domain in which human uncertainty is most extreme. Once his basic needs are satisfied (indeed, sometimes even before), man is subject to intense desires, though he may not know precisely for what. The reason is that he desires *being*, something he himself lacks and which some other person seems to possess. The subject thus looks to that other person to inform him of what he should desire in order to acquire that being. If the model, who is apparently already endowed with superior being, desires some object, that object must surely be capable of conferring an even greater plenitude of being.[71]

---

69. *The Way to Freedom* (San Francisco: Harper, 1994), 130.

70. *Things Hidden since the Foundation of the World*, trans. Stephen Bann and Michael Metteer (Stanford, Calif.: Stanford University Press, 1977), 441.

71. Quoted in *Violence and the Sacred*, trans. Patrick Gregory (Baltimore: Johns Hopkins University Press, 1977), 145–46.

This model of human nature explains why children often don't want to play with a toy until another child expresses interest in it and, on a larger scale, why individuals compete to possess the same symbols of status and success. Such competition can quickly degenerate into a war of all against all, as imitation of the desires of others leads to rivalry and sometimes even to fratricide.

For Girard, such a crisis is mitigated through the identification and killing of a scapegoat. At some point, instead of violence being directed at everyone in general and no one in particular, it is focused on a specific victim who is singled out by some uniqueness or weakness. In the collective murder of this victim, the violence of all against all ends, and a human community emerges.

The killing of a single chosen victim provides the means for the formation of social cohesion. Personal desires are transformed into a collective desire to defeat the projected evil, which is then resolved by the destruction of someone designated as the source of that evil. Then a "myth" is erected to bless that sacrifice as divine, and to justify the violence as a necessary act and its perpetrators as heroes. For Girard this sacred violence is the origin of all human societies and all cultural mythologies. It is at once the fall and the ascension of man.

The community then seeks to recreate this feeling again and again through the reenactment of the original murder in sacred rituals and by the substitution of new victims for the original victim. Each time this ritual is repeated, the distance from the original murder becomes greater, and contemporary acts of persecution become more diffuse and symbolic, until a new act of sacred violence is called forth to revivify the fading mythology and give renewed "moral" authority to the group.

Girard's research into the ubiquitous nature of the scapegoat phenomenon in myth and literature ultimately led him to a religious conversion when he came to the conclusion that the story of the scapegoat as retold in the Gospels demythologizes the religious justification for persecution. The Gospels tell the story of violence against the scapegoat from the standpoint of the victim. That is to say, they make it clear that God is on the side of the victimized, not the self-righteous community. As such, they expose the myths that justify violence as pious frauds.

By focusing attention on the victim, the Bible undermines the psychological power of the scapegoat mechanism. As Girard puts it, "Once understood, the mechanisms can no longer operate; we believe less and less in the culpability of the victims they demand. Deprived of the food that sustains them, the institutions derived from these mechanisms collapse one after the other around us. Whether we know it or not, the Gospels are responsible for this collapse."[72] This revelation—or *kerygma*—is echoed and confirmed in the Old Testament prophets: truth does not lie on the side of the crowd, but on the side of the oppressed, the poor, the exiled, and the abandoned.

The difference between Girard and traditional Christian apologists is that he links the debunking of the scapegoat myth in the crucifixion of Christ to a philosophical anthropology of revelation that synthesizes sociology, theology, and culture studies within a single overall theory of human nature. From Girard's perspective, however, the common Christian understanding of the cross, as a vicarious atonement, is a reversion of Christianity to sacrificial thinking. Such a lapse falls away from the good news of the New Testament and turns Christianity into just another scapegoat myth that justifies holy violence in defense of the faith.

Yet Girard has no desire to make historical Christianity itself into a scapegoat. Eugene Webb in his book *The Self Between* describes Girard's views.

> Misleading as it has been, Girard considers historical Christianity, too, to have played a needed, if ironic, role in preserving the gospel of Christ. When Christianity spread in the ancient world to vast numbers of people who had no deep knowledge of the biblical tradition and its progressive critique of sacred violence, the sacrificial version of Christianity served to make it acceptable to them and thereby to preserve, like a protective envelope, the buried traces of the real message of Christ until a time would come when its true meaning

72. Quoted in Gerald J. Bieseker-Mast, "Reading René Girard's and Walter Wink's Religious Critiques of Violence as Radical Communication Ethics," a speech delivered November 20–23, 1997, at the annual meeting of the Communication Association. Available online at www.bluffton.edu/~mastg/Girard.htm.

could be grasped. Girard believes that with the development of modern psychological and sociological insights and the contemporary entry of lived history into apocalyptic conditions, the time for that long awaited unveiling has now come. What will be specifically unveiled, he believes, besides the mimetic and victimizing mechanisms, is the real meaning of the invitation to life that Jesus delivered. This is above all an invitation to share fully in the life that Jesus shared with the Father, a life of nonviolent love.[73]

In this sense Girard is both prophet and apologist, refiguring the Christian revelation in the language of contemporary social science while at the same time articulating the challenges that Christian thought presents to conventional notions of desire, violence, and civilization. His work has inspired thinkers across a multitude of disciplines.

Eric Gans in his book *Signs of Paradox* explains the entire field of generative anthropology as having emerged out of Girard's understanding of the human. Generative anthropology, Gans tells us, is not a methodology but an attempt to understand culture while remaining "always attentive to the human, understood as the paradoxical generation of the transcendent from the immanent, the vertical from the horizontal."[74] It is an attempt "to understand human origin as the pivotal event that invents and discovers both crisis and paradox, crisis as the realization of paradox, paradox as the solution to crisis."[75] Human culture, in the Girardian sense, Gans tells us, is the deferral of violence through representation.[76]

If Girard is right, then Christian symbology is more than just another religious system; it is the key to exposing the violence inherent within any and all world mythologies and hence has the potential to end the cycle of retribution that animates world history. After Christ's death on the cross, mankind can no longer kid itself that power over others is divinely justified, and this makes all the excuses for murder, oppression, and unjust social hierarchies obsolete.

73. Eugene Webb, *The Self Between* (Seattle: University of Washington Press, 1993), 187.
74. Eric Gans, *Signs of Paradox* (Stanford, Calif.: Stanford University Press, 1997), 4.
75. Ibid.
76. Ibid., 5.

If Girard is right, if his philosophical anthropology of mimetic desire does in fact reflect the dynamics of the human condition, then we are all, at this very moment, living in a post-Girardian age, a civilization on the far side of all world mythologies. And even though our behavior and our politics, and even our awareness, have yet to catch up with what he has revealed, everything we do, think, say, and believe lies under its judgment.

All victims are now analogues for the Christ; all victimizers representatives of Pilate. Morality is thus freed from its search for blame to a recognition of our shared responsibility in the social perpetuation of evil. The dispersal of power is rendered transparent without establishing any teleological or utopian high ground for anybody. Atonement is accomplished not through official channels—secular, religious or otherwise—but through a recognition that it has already been achieved. Evil is always extending mankind's worship of power and control, while the good is always extending its adherence to conscience whatever its "worldly" consequences.

This is why, for Girard, the resurrection of the body presents a counter-image to both the untethered spiritualism of the Gnostics and the tragic worldview of the stoics, both of whom deny the social effectiveness of the freely given gift. It is an image reconciling the inner and outer, the Other and the Same, and the living with the dead, thereby providing us with an image of history overcome, significance dispersed throughout all of creation, and power taken out of the hands of the few and returned to the many. The Trinity now stands for a postdialectical understanding of Being that cannot be subsumed within any binary system. Pure Gift. Pure Love. Pure Presence. Absolute relationship.

Girard makes clear that once we see that our self-justifications and personal sense of morality are largely psychological maneuvers to avoid such deep responsibility and profound love—and once the ubiquitous nature of the psychology of the scapegoat is revealed to be at the heart of all societies, all faiths, and all cultural mythologies—we can never again destroy another human being in good faith. Never again can the state cloak its violence in the false cloth of morality, and never again can love of country or revolution justify violence. We might still choose to participate in those things, but God does not.

The truth of God's unconditional love for all his creation has been made clear, and all of us are now responsible to God over and above the demands of history while living in history! A universal morality now stands before us like the angel at the tomb. And though this knowledge won't end violence or war or even scapegoating, it will end their moral sanction, and that in itself is the beginning of the end to mankind's unconscious slavery to evil. Just as Nietzsche had exposed the "Death of God" before those living in it understood his critique or saw through their own illusory values, so too do we stand in the aftermath of the end of all world mythologies, still half believing in the possibility of self-justification.

But if Girard is right, the game is up, and we can now begin to understand the bizarre political history of the twentieth century by acknowledging that "normality" is pathological—that a profound sickness lies inherent within the very structure of civilization. Our ordinary selves have been revealed to be one with the violence of society itself, and to the extent we place our love of family or country or even religion above our love of truth, we will continue to thwart the divine will until the utter amorality of our actions convicts us before the postmythological God of actuality whose victim-Messiah has already made it abundantly clear that all we ever needed to stand in right relationship to him was to love our neighbor as ourselves.

5

The Role of the Christian Mysteries
in the Life of the Modern Mind

There comes a time when civilization has to be renewed
by the discovery of new mysteries, by the undemocratic
but sovereign power of the imagination, by the undemo-
cratic power which makes poets the unacknowledged legisla-
tors of mankind, the power which makes all things new.

Norman O. Brown, "The Place of Mystery in the Life of the Mind"[1]

When I say I believe, I do not mean that I take over for myself
what the Church says on these matters (God, Trinity, Incarnation,
Redemption, and Eucharist) but that through Love I hold on to the
perfect unseizable truth which these mysteries contain, and that I
try to open my soul to it so that its light may penetrate into me.

Simone Weil, *Gateway to God*[2]

1. Norman O. Brown, "The Place of Mystery in the Life of the Mind," *Harper's Magazine,* May 1961, 46–49.
2. Simone Weil, *Gateway to God* (Glasgow: Collins, 1974), 72.

What we see in the contemporary Christian avant-garde is what we have always seen in Christian thinkers: a working through of their ambivalent relationship to their world, their times, and themselves—coupled with a radical skepticism toward their own human capacities. Slavoj Zizek writes:

> Christianity asserts as the highest act precisely what pagan wisdom condemns as the source of Evil: the gesture of *separation,* of drawing the line, of clinging to an element that disturbs the balance of All. The pagan criticism that the Christian insight is not "deep enough," that it fails to grasp the primordial One-All, therefore misses the point: Christianity *is* the miraculous Event that disturbs the balance of the One-All; it *is* the violent intrusion of Difference that precisely throws the balanced circuit of the universe off the rails.[3]

In other words, Christian thought critiques mainstream culture but also sees itself under judgment; our best modern Christian intellectuals have turned thinking against themselves into a veritable art: from Blake to Dostoyevsky, from Kierkegaard to Chesterton, all the way to Dorothy Day and Walker Percy, the exemplary mode of modern Christian thought has been a triadic structure of self-reflection, paradox, and irony that reverses the values of this world and the logic of cause and effect.

The difference between the orthodox mysteries and the Gnostic mysteries is that the orthodox mysteries are not really mysteries at all but doctrines held back from the uninitiated so that they will not be misunderstood or reduced to cheap approximations. Orthodox Christianity is a set of ideas and postulates that have to be mastered, and the initiate has to join a Christian community if he or she is to truly grasp the experiential wisdom they express.

The incarnation and the resurrection are, as Blake reminded us, visionary realities not reducible to the categories of space and time. What they

---

3. Slavoj Zizek, *The Fragile Absolute, or, Why Is the Christian Legacy Worth Fighting For?* (London and New York: Verso, 2000), 214.

mean has more to do with God's omniscience, love, and transcendence than with any ideas that one must "believe." They are, in other words, enabling concepts, not positivist metaphysical absolutes.

But once Christians are initiated, God ceases to be a concept and reincarnates himself as the conscience of their conscience. And when the supernatural meaning of the Gospels becomes transparent through this transformation, reason no longer appears to be the enemy of faith, but its servant and guide.

In our time Christianity has become one of the more useful speculative philosophical anthropologies; it's spirituality, a progressive form of experimental psychology and it's ecclesiology, a model of redeemed statecraft. If "dialectics" raises thought to the second power by factoring the logic of our thinking into the content of our thoughts, then Christianity has the potential to raise thought to the third power by not only factoring in the relationship of meaning to method but also the relationship of meaning and method to the mysterious entity that unites them: the thinker of the thought, the soul of the self.

The reason that Walker Percy, following the insights of Charles Sanders Peirce, contrasted *triadic* structures to dyadic ones and that René Girard posited a *three*-pronged relationship at the heart of human desire is that both of them needed some way to explain the radically unpredictable nature of human subjectivity. By positing a third "player" and the existence of an invisible, immaterial "coupler" that unites sign and sense, it became possible to think about language not only as a form of behavior or as a system of signs conditioned by historical and economic realities, but as an expression of the self, and therefore as a vehicle not only of information but also of irrationality, anarchy, lies, fictions, and myths. The experience of a trinitarian model of human communication makes it possible to talk systematically about contingency, angst, and moral confusion without having to explain them away as mere epiphenomena of simpler structures of cause and effect.

In his book *Intellectuals,* Paul Johnson exposed the personal problems many modern thinkers have returning from the dyadic world of abstract ideas and cause-and-effect relationships to the triadic structures and immanent realities of their own personal lives. Their commitment to scientific explanations of reality allows them to make breakthroughs in the realm of science but does not translate well to the triadic realms of interpersonal relationships. This often leaves our greatest minds frustrated with common existence and prone to psychological inflation, narcissism, megalomania, bohemianism, and the consolations of vice. The psychology of the Unabomber is, perhaps, more of a universal "type" than many "intellectuals" would care to admit.

To illustrate this, Walker Percy uses the example of the Los Alamos scientist whose wife sued him for divorce, claiming that during the day the scientist and his colleague may have been probing the mysteries of the natural universe according to the most refined protocols of empirical science, but when he came home at night, he was miserly, self-indulgent, and belligerent, and spent his evenings drinking beer and watching television. Nothing in his scientific training argued against such behavior; in fact, it even helped to explain it away as essentially irrelevant in the larger scheme of things. In this scientist's world, his wife's subjectivity was not a cosmos to be entered so much as an object to be dealt with like everything else.[4]

Science (or any other autonomous discipline) does not solve the problems of the self or the riddles of life. It barely even acknowledges the existence of human subjectivity—except as the daunting "problem" of consciousness. Not that Christian thinkers are immune to any of these problems. The self-deceived, hypocritical preacher is also a Western archetype. But at least the triadic understanding of the dynamics of the human person implicit in the Christian worldview acknowledges the need for a third party to mediate our experiences. And though Christians may not always recognize their true place in the cosmos, they are less likely to embrace the delusion that they have transcended conventional existence altogether and are, therefore, free from "petty" obligations and common

4. Walker Percy, *Lost in the Cosmos*, 124–26.

morality. In other words, Christians aren't better than other people, but their worldview encourages them to recognize that fact.

For Christian thinkers, eschatology affirms an end that hasn't yet arrived and so isn't yet understood. Unlike the teleologies of Hegel and Marx or the endlessness of Nietzsche's eternal return, the Christian image of the end challenges them to constantly rethink and reimagine their place in the ultimate scheme of things, "for what is our end but to reach that Kingdom that has no end."[5]

The promise of the resurrection of the body forces them to question reductionist materialist metaphysics or any view that cancels out the individual. It challenges them to imagine a cosmos where the living are one with the dead, the past one with the future, and the eternal one with the temporal.

Christian thinkers, of the kind I am examining here, aren't all that interested in defending their faith, so much as seizing upon revealed reality in its highest expectation and tension toward the future. Their thinking is not strictly speaking "apologetics" but something more engaged—an attempt to "say" what the world looks like as seen through eyes transformed by an encounter with the living God. In other words, Christian scholarship is *witness*—not necessarily of doctrinal or dogmatic truths but of the concrete realities made visible through a belief in them. It is the product of a sensibility detached from worldly ambitions and nurtured by an intellectual freedom that grows out of the gratuitousness of love.

For them, the kingdom has already come, so the shadow side of things—the injustices, the perversity, indeed the implacable reality of sin in all its endless variations—is not something to be particularly worried about or capitulated to. Theirs is not a "warrior politics" or a "pagan ethos" like the kind advocated by Robert D. Kaplan, who sees nothing wrong with exploiting others' weaknesses in order to accomplish "great things."[6] Like their prophetic and Romantic precursors, "the orthodox

5. This famous line is from the conclusion of Saint Augustine's *City of* God, trans. Henry Bettenson (New York: Penguin, 1984), 1091.

6. See Robert D. Kaplan, *Warrior Politics: Why Leadership Demands a Pagan Ethos* (New York: Random House, 2002).

avant-garde" want to give hope to the hopeless and pause to the proud. Yet they are also radically suspicious of their own motives and assumptions, suspecting themselves almost as much as their adversaries, loving their crooked neighbor with their own crooked hearts.

Theodore Adorno was getting at this paradox when he remarked that "only insofar as culture withdraws from Man can it be faithful to him."[7] That is to say, only when culture questions our natural impulses, rather than serves them, is it useful to humanity. But what separates Christian scholars from Adorno is their *a priori* commitment to the Gospel message that the kingdom has *already been established* and that the Lord of truth is indeed risen and reigning over it. So they simply assume the unity of truth, the goodness of creation, the divine origin of all things, and the illusory nature of our "felt" separation from others and from God. The intellectual heroism of religious thought does not come from its willingness to imaginatively transcend the human condition, but from its willingness to accept its own limitations knowing full well that these limitations are more a symptom of mankind's incapacity than they are of God's.

The Christian mysteries, therefore, contradict and expose the dogmas of modernism in at least five important ways.

1. They throw doubt upon all reductionist explanations of human life and behavior—especially the modern dogma of psychological "motivism"—the idea that human actions are motivated by relatively simple drives toward self-preservation or personal gain of one kind or another. Christian novelists especially see this as a narrow and misguided view of human nature and interrogate it with a philosophical anthropology born of the Gospels and the Sermon on the Mount.

Our so-called motivated selves are not our *true selves* but our *fallen* or *false selves* that mirror an incomplete understanding of the human condition. We can transcend these illusory identities only through repentance and grace, but this is never anything we ourselves can control

7. Theodore Adorno, *Politics and Aesthetics,* trans. Ronald Taylor (London: Verso, 1977), 23.

or dictate. The terms are set by God alone. The meaning of our actions and the content of our experience are not defined by material history. We are all equally loved, equally lost, equally open to redemption inside a reality that transcends time and change.

2. They confirm the novelists' suspicion that we are not existentially cut off from everybody and everything else—affirming the *good news* that we are already One. We haven't yet grasped the full implications of this revelation because our imaginations are dominated by superficial "differences"—an error exacerbated by modern political ideologies.

3. They challenge the modern assumption of a value-free universe and propose instead a cosmos in the throes of a deeply partisan struggle in which good triumphs over evil, justice over injustice, and love over hate. We do not live in a moral vacuum, but inside an ongoing struggle to spiritualize existence. The activists of the heart examined here, from Dorothy Day and Martin Luther King Jr. to Thomas Merton and Wendell Berry, carry this revelation to the forefront of their thought and challenge all of us to live up to its full implications.

4. But perhaps the most striking challenge to the modern imagination leveled by the Christian mysteries is their rejection of the notion that the scientific method is the best and only way of knowing. This is exposed most clearly by Christian macrohistorians who argues that even though science has exposed the distortions of "magical thinking" and unfounded metaphysical speculation, its pursuit of irrefutable, demonstrable "truth" often leads to a disinterest in the provisional, refutable, existential "truths" that communities, cultures, and individuals need to agree upon every day simply to exist.

Wayne C. Booth points out that the struggle to find common ground is sorely lacking in the modern world, and he contrasts this search for sharable ideas and beliefs—what he calls "the rhetoric of assent"—to the epistemology of science, especially to Karl Popper's doctrine of "falsification," which argues that the best way to understand the world is to actively seek out evidence that can falsify our theories in pursuit of an irrefutable vision of reality. This approach works very well to eliminate bogus attributions of cause and effect and to further the natural sciences, but it doesn't really help us to find "reasons" to work together or to come to common agreement on the relatively arbitrary projects and creative endeavors that constitute most of what human beings do every day.[8]

By defining thinking as refutation, modern science has remade modern culture into its own skeptical image, and this has proven to be a problem, especially in democratic societies, where experts have come to replace citizens as the final public authority.

This shifts the locus of debate from who we are, what we should want, and where we should be going to what we can *know* for sure and what we can make happen. These are not the most important questions to ask in any given circumstance. They are certainly not the questions posed by Marshall McLuhan to explain the effects of modern media on our lives or by René Girard to explain the human proclivity to violence or by Jacques Ellul to explain the hidden psychological and moral impact of technology.

5. The final modern dogma incompatible with the Christian mysteries has to do with the *ends of culture* and the purposes of argument. Modern science gives us power over the world, whereas the Christian mysteries hold us accountable for our stewardship of the earth and our attempts to establish "the beloved community." That is to say, Christianity teaches that the purpose of life and thought is love, not power.

I can best explain this distinction with an example. Many years ago, just after Mother Teresa had been awarded the Nobel Prize, she was on a Canadian interview show with a biologist who had also just won a Nobel Prize. During the discussion, the biologist began to speak of the possibility of creating everlasting life through DNA research. To stir things up, the host asked Mother Teresa what she thought of the possibility of "real" everlasting life as opposed to the church "fiction." Mother Teresa replied, "I believe in love and compassion." It was one of those moments

8. See Wayne C. Booth's unsung minor masterpiece *Modern Dogma and the Rhetoric of Assent* (Notre Dame, Ind.: Notre Dame University Press, 1974).

when the narrow ambitions, self-centeredness, pride, and delusions of our modern civilization were seen through, and an issue reframed in the light of a transcendent perspective that simply bypassed all modern dogmas, prejudices, and half-truths. Would everlasting life matter if one lived in a world without love and compassion?

After the show, the biologist admitted that Mother Teresa's comment had taken him as close as he had ever come to religious conversion.

Conclusion

*What solution is there? There is no answer to this collective syn-
drome of a whole culture, this fascination, this mad whirl of denial
of otherness, of all strangeness, all negativity, this repudiation of
evil and reconciliation around the selfsame and its multiple figures:
incest, autism, twinship, cloning. We can only remember that seduc-
tion resides in the safeguarding of alien-ness, in non-reconciliation.
One should not be reconciled with one's body, nor with oneself,
one should not be reconciled with the other, one should not be
reconciled with nature, one should not reconcile male and female
nor good and evil. Therein lies the secret of a strange attraction.*

Jean Baudrillard[1]

*You do not enter paradise tomorrow, or the day after, or in ten
years, you enter it today when you are poor and crucified.*

Leon Bloy[2]

The point that many moderns fail to grasp about Christian thinkers
is that they have very little interest in changing the world. They seek
merely to see things clearly in the light of God's hidden logic. And if, by

1. Jean Baudrillard, *The Perfect Crime*, trans. Chris Turner (London: Verso, 1996), 129–30.
2. Bloy, *Pilgrim of the Absolute*, 10.

so doing, they expose the narcissism of their contemporaries, the false agendas of their leaders, and the didactic pornography of their artists and entertainers—well, that is all to the good. But unlike their more utilitarian peers, they desire to *live in the truth* even more than they desire *to be effective in the world*, and this puts them on the far side of a very important and a very deep intellectual divide: it puts them in the camp of the stoic poor, the moral outcasts, and the political and literary pariahs.

Solutions to life's dilemmas are a dime a dozen, sold on every street corner, and proffered by every pundit from Washington, D.C., to the suburbs of Basra, Iraq. Each and every one of them has a solution to the world's problems, usually involving the shedding of someone else's blood. But for the Christian critics examined here, injustice is not something that can ever be defeated. It must be constantly combated. When it disappears in one place, it reappears in another. Abuse migrates, disguises itself as virtue, and then moves on. We can never isolate evil, because it isn't a system or a person or party. If it were, it could be gotten rid of permanently—which is the dream of all totalizing philosophers and world conquerors.

But evil manifests itself more in an *absence* of care, in an *absence* of perception, and in the negation of Being than it does in the *presence* of stupidity, violence, or even hatred. It is more often than not a species of folly—a commitment to "virtues" that are not really virtues. And so no procedure or method can ever identify it or completely defeat it because it masks itself in the guise of goodness, justice, necessary reforms, and even scientific objectivity. It wears a suit or a uniform, waves a flag, and has credentials. This is why the primary moral task from a Christian perspective is first to *perceive evil*. And this requires that one see what isn't there and through the things that are. This is possible only for someone who is suspicious of virtue and believes in a reality greater than his own.

What the Christian mysteries require from us is not that we construct a better world, but that we love and serve the one we are given. As one Parisian graffiti artist wrote in 1968, "the intellectuals have hitherto only changed the world; the point is to understand it." This is a decidedly contemplative observation, one that confirms Blake's suspicions of the new activism and Kierkegaard's view that even if someone could speak the Word of God directly today, no one in the modern world could hear it, simply because there is too much noise and distraction. The function of the modern apostle, therefore, is to create the silent, contemplative spaces where individuals can experience the truth for themselves.

Technology, modern science, and political activism all run counter to this contemplative tradition, for they cannot comprehend the possibility that it is precisely when one is most successful and in control of one's life that one is most likely in the grip of an illusion. Evil makes great use of the human mind because practical intelligence always dwells on re-sults, not first premises or ultimate ends. To make certainty our highest intellectual standard, or success the measure of our ideas, is to still the dissenting wisdom of the heart and thereby blind the soul to alternative possibilities and life's abiding ironies.

The thinkers examined in this book—if they have done nothing else—have shifted the axes of inquiry away from the search for certainty back to the religious quest for ontological vibrancy and prophetic insight. In their work, the high cultural criticism born of Western rationalism finds its complement and critique in the Judeo-Christian prophetic tradition of poetic vision and social dissent. Judged by purely rational standards, there are many questions about the validity of Kierkegaard's philosophy, the accuracy of Blake's visions, and even the literary skill of Dostoyevsky as a novelist. But once one adopts prophetic religious categories and standards, Kierkegaard's criticism of Hegelian ontology is unquestion-ably revelatory, Blake's transcendence of "realist" aesthetics liberating, and Dostoyevsky's transformation of the novel into secular scripture: a moral, philosophical, and literary breakthrough.

This shift in perspective from epistemological certainty to transforma-tional revelation turns the tables on modernism and reveals an alterna-tive tradition within Western thought: a tradition keyed to what Boris Pasternak called "the history within history." That is to say, by refocusing our concerns back on the intertwining destinies of individual human lives (as opposed to general laws and collective trends), we come to see ourselves as part of a very personal and very sacred set of enterprises, not as atoms in an inhumane evolutionary process or pawns in some international game of chess. This tension between the sacred self and its historical circumstances is the very theme and content of the Bible and at the heart of the role the Christian mysteries play in the life of the mind: they foreground conscience and downplay worldliness, admonishing us to attend to the higher worth and calling of our own unique individual lives rather than to the lesser good of getting what we think we want.

With this book, I had originally set out to write a survey of creative contemporary Christian scholarship—what I called "the orthodox avant-garde." My goal was simply to demonstrate that it was possible to begin from religious, *even sectarian,* premises and yet arrive at nonpartisan, even universal, insights into the human condition. A religious world-view—indeed a Christian worldview—need not blind one to contemporary realities; indeed, it should lead one to even greater objectivity and critical distance from the fashions, fads, and assumptions of our day. This was certainly true for artistic and intellectual innovators such as Andy Warhol, John Coltrane, Marshall McLuhan, and Ivan Illich.

But as I proceeded in my inquiry, I discovered a more unified contemplative Christian anthropology than I had ever imagined, one spearheaded by René Girard's critique of the scapegoat and flanked by a whole cadre of twentieth-century religious social critics Dorothy Day, Thomas Merton, Jacques Ellul, and E. F. Schumacher, and novelists like Dostoyevsky, Pasternak, Kerouac, and Percy. This emergent religious countermodernism offer an explicit alternative to positivist religion, science, literature, and ethics, and offers a way to resolve the classical antinomies that continue to plague postmodern thought.

We now know that the so-called absolutes of Christianity lie outside any particular cultural expressions of them, and yet, paradoxically, those very same "absolutes" can only be embodied in those relative expressions. This makes modern Christian thinkers paradoxicalists by definition. On the one hand, they see through all world mythologies as products of particular places and times, and yet, at the same time, they acknowledge a transcultural Absolute that unites all of humanity in a shared participation with the divine. In other words, religious modernists (or postmoderns, if you prefer) never lose sight of the fact that they are *in* this world, but not *of* it, inside prevailing descriptions of reality but not defined by them. And this realization makes for a very different kind of cultural criticism—a cultural criticism that is as aware of its own tragic limitations as it is of its power to see through common illusions.

Kant's four questions—Who am I? What can I know? What ought I do? What dare I hope?—reflect Enlightenment concerns with self-conception, certainty, moral will, and fulfillment, concerns our civilization continues to take seriously and put at the center of its political and cultural agenda. But in a post-Kantian context, these are no longer the primary issues. And so it is little matter if Hegel, Marx, Popper, or, for that matter, Heidegger or Wittgenstein *solved them*. Technological developments have shifted the ontological question to "Who am I *this time?*" and the epistemological question of "What can I know?" into "What world is this?" The "old" modern ethical issue "What ought I do?" has become "What ought I do *this time, in this context?*" And the religious question of "What dare I hope?" has now become "What dare I hope *in this particular world?*"

Life has become so historically and culturally contextualized that it is increasingly experienced as psychologically, linguistically, and even ontologically random. The contemplative Christian thinkers examined here get outside the Kantian philosophical universe of discourse (and hence contemporary confusion) by going back to a largely wordless awareness of the Absolute that predates the modern experience of contingency, relativity, and radical mobility. Hence, they are not particularly concerned with finding stability or establishing a coherent social order, because they have discovered a divine order transcendent to the concerns of this world.

If, in our time, ontology has been replaced by transpersonal psychology, epistemology by the sociology of knowledge, ethics by the dynamics of self-realization, and religion by the politics of meaning, the new Christian humanists examined here reveal all these changes as half measures. The old "new" world is fading, and at the very moment of its eclipse, form and field have exchanged places. Just as the classical, atomized self has been seen through, a new interiority has emerged, and our traditions have come back to us historicized and clarified.

The postmodern temptation is to identify with the mind that authored this critique, but this "self" is just as unreal as the old one, another illusion produced by the wheel of time with its endless alterities between sign and system, self and cosmos. The Christian contemplative critics tell us that our true self is beyond all this: in that place where we are one, that place where the macrohistorians stand when they survey the unfolding expanse of human time, and where the poets and the novelists go to pen their dialogic epics on the ironies of destiny, and where our great social activists are martyred.

Fifty years from now, the post-Kantian questions now dominating this generation of scholars will have disappeared along with their sense of intellectual urgency. Who knows what will replace them or what kind of "life" and what kind of "issues" will dominate in the years to come? Jean Baudrillard speculates that future anthropologists may someday (if the world continues down the path of epistemological skepticism and radical doubt) look upon every common object from our era as a religious artifact from a world that once believed it was *real*. They will marvel at our credulity, at how we believed in the superstitions of self, nation, body, nature, love, and history. Such is the way the future will dispense with us, alter *life*, discount our experience, and reframe itself as primary.

But the thinkers examined here offer us an escape from this one-way ticket to oblivion by way of an eschatological perspective on existence (as opposed to a merely evolutionary one). For them, the final things are the first things, and the first things are love, hope, and charity. Secular human history is largely the record of partial beings narrating their own illusory progress toward imaginary self-sufficiency. But true life is not encompassed by such narrow narratives. Like the beloved community, it can only be discovered, not made.

At the very moment civilizations seem to be colliding, our inner lives have begun an unforeseen return to sources, to silence, to humility, to asceticism, and to the deep listening that is known as contemplation. Beyond the impasses of critical theory, inside the paradoxes of the real, on the surfaces of the simulacra, and at the very limits of negative dialectics, stands religion unbowed, but powerless to explain its own survival.

We are, and have been for many years, in a shift from modernist ambition to millennial contrition. All our conflicts with others and with ourselves have been the product of our unacknowledged conflicts with the Absolute. Martin Heidegger once defined being as "the presence-ing of absence through time." This is a startlingly poetic way of describing the human condition, but we have to go back to a Christian cosmology to pick up on it. It's true: we are *absences* present to ourselves, what Augustine described as empty vessels seeking to be filled by God. Idolatry is simply the attempt to fill these vessels with what is at hand; it is, if you will, a desire to be complete before we have been completed. And here is the odd and challenging turn in the postmodern version of the Christian revelation: God does not *fill* us with himself, because God is not Being, not Essence, not any "thing." He is that *which is coming into Being;* that is to say: God is *beginning* or God is *relationship.* You can say it either way.

The great christological insight is that the false self seeks meaning in a perpetual growing out of itself through achievement, acquisitions, and expressions of the will, whereas the true self finds solace in the stability of truth. Truth not as power over nature, but as coherence, unity, and comprehension.

In this sense, faith is a cosmos, a psychological and spiritual space for knowing and experiencing God. Without this inner laboratory of prayer or the presencing of our absence in time, we simply cannot experience ourselves as anything other than organisms not long for this world. But once we acknowledge the gift of "presence" and share it with other "absences," we become not only wounded healers (as Father Henri Nouwen once described Christian apostleship), but what Rainer Rilke called "bees of the invisible," spiritual scouts living at the edge of culture, members in residence of the orthodox avant-garde surveying the ever expanding geography of the soul.

Seen from this perspective, spiritual growth is largely a process of dismantling false identifications, cognitive distortions, and idolatrous conceptions. We moderns—heirs to powerful world-conquering techniques—are not particularly good at this. We live largely on the surfaces of things, pragmatic to a fault and alive primarily to the images directly before us. We have a difficult time imagining the spiritual side of culture that takes apart illusions and dispenses with false virtues and socially victorious half-truths. Finding our way back to a contemplative existence may require us to follow the unlikely paths of the literary imagination and the lost traditions of prayer.

Jean Baudrillard once described our contemporary situation in a way that reflects the ontological dissent of our best religious thinkers:

> Existence is something we must not consent to. It has been given to us as a consolation prize, and we must not believe in it. The will is something we must not consent to. It has been given to us as the illusion of an autonomous subject. Now, if there is anything worse than being subject to the law of others, it is surely being subject to one's own law. The real is something we must not consent to. It has been given to us as simulacrum, and the worst thing is to believe in it for want of anything else. The only thing we should consent to is the rule. But in that case, we are speaking not of the rule of the subject, but the rule of the way of the world.[3]

The thinkers examined here would undoubtedly agree, but they would point out that there is another rule: the Rule of St. Benedict. And that in the monastic life, we see a synthesis of distributist economics combined with a metahistorical critique. Thomas Merton went a long way in bringing that rule into dialogue with our times, but we lay Christians must cross the bridge he built from the secular side of the divide. This means using the contributions of our most progressive thinkers and art-

3. Baudrillard, *Perfect Crime*, 11.

ists as harbingers of an as-yet-to-be-realized, international, contemplative counterculture.

There are many secret places in the soul, many lost passages and hidden stairways, but in order to get to them, we must first pass through the doors of visionary perception. The real story of our time is not the tragedy of clashing civilizations or the philosophical narrative of the end of ideology; it is more accurately the global epic of estranged pagans—ourselves included—rediscovering their spiritual lives.

We are all—East and West, First and Third World, male and female—spiritual exiles to a greater or lesser extent, who have lived far too long in the land of the Philistines, drinking the Pharaoh's wine. To free ourselves, we need a counter-environment (if only in our heads) that will allow us to detach from this world long enough to see through its self-satisfied commonplaces. The cutting-edge Christian writers, thinkers, and artists examined here provide us with the critical tools to do just that. We would be foolish not to follow their lead. But they are only a beginning. I began this essay with a parable from Elie Wiesel. Let me end with one from Jean-Luc Godard.

In his sci-fi film *Alphaville,* the world is ruled by a supercomputer. The last free man, "Lemmy Caution" (a rough melding of Albert Camus and Humphrey Bogart), is the only person the master computer cannot figure out or control, so every so often he is called in for an interrogation. Lemmy answers all the computer's questions with lines from modernist poetry. For example, the computer might ask him where he has been, and he'd reply with something like, "I've been scuttling along the floors of silent seas."

At one point in the interrogation, Lemmy asks the computer, in effect, "Why don't you just leave me alone? You will never understand me." (I am translating *very loosely* here!)

The computer replies that man underestimates the power of artificial intelligence and that he has already catalogued thousands of Lemmy's metaphors. How many more could he have?

Lemmy replies (and I am going way beyond translation here into my own interpretation) that once the computer grasps the meaning of metaphor, he will then understand that language is an expression of human freedom, not merely a tool for cognition or calculation, and that once he grasps that, he will cease being a computer and become a human being. And once he becomes a human being, he will then know that love and freedom matter more than power, and he will set Lemmy free.

The computer mulls this over for a second, then suggests they continue the interrogation next week. And so the conversation goes on, between the machines who would be humans and the humans who refuse to become machines. But it isn't *really* a dialogue, just a staying action, an impasse in the war between the living and the dead, and an attempt by the soul to keep revelation in the game until the next great leap forward.

Works Cited

Adorno, Theodore. *Minima Moralia*. Trans. E. F. N. Jephcott. Frankfurt: Suhrkamp, 1951.

_____. *Politics and Aesthetics*. Trans. Ronald Taylor. London: Verso, 1977.

Altizer, Thomas J. J. *The New Apocalypse: The Radical Christian Vision of William Blake*. East Lansing: Michigan State University Press, 1967.

_____with William Hamilton. *Radical Theology and the Death of God*. Indianapolis: Bobbs-Merrill, 1966.

Arendt, Hannah. *Men in Dark Times*. New York: Harcourt Brace Jovanovich, 1970.

Augustine of Hippo, St. *City of God*. Trans. Henry Bettenson. New York: Penguin, 1984 [1091].

Baudrillard, Jean. *Forget Foucault*. New York: Semiotexte, 1987.

_____. *The Perfect Crime*. Trans. Chris Turner. London: Verso, 1996.

Becker, Ernst. *The Denial of Death*. New York: The Free Press, 1973.

Berdyaev, Nicholas. *The Meaning of History*. Trans. George Reavey. Cleveland: Meridian Books, 1962.

Berry, Wendell. *Another Turn of the Crank*. New York: Counterpoint, 1996.

_____. *Citizenship Papers*. Washington, D.C.: Shoemaker & Hoard, 2003.

_____. *In the Presence of Fear: Three Essays for a Changed World*. Great Barrington, Mass.: Orion Society, 2001.

_____. *Life Is a Miracle*. Washington, D.C.: Counterpoint, 2000.

Blake, William. *Poetry and Prose of William Blake*. Ed. Geoffrey Keynes. London: Nonesuch Library, 1961.

_____. *The Selected Poetry and Prose of William Blake.* Ed. Northrop Frye. New York: Modern Library, 1953.

Bloom, Allan. *The Closing of the American Mind.* New York: Simon & Schuster, 1988.

Bloom, Harold. *Breaking the Vessels.* Chicago: University of Chicago Press, 1982.

_____. *Kabbalah and Criticism.* New York: Continuum, 1975.

_____. *Omens of Millennium.* New York: Riverhead Books, 1997.

Bloy, Léon. *Pilgrim of the Absolute.* Ed. Raïssa Maritain. Trans. John Coleman and Harry Lorin Binsse. London: Eyre and Spottiswoode, 1947.

Booth, Wayne C. *Modern Dogma and the Rhetoric of Assent.* Notre Dame, Ind.; Notre Dame University Press, 1974.

Branch, Taylor. *Parting the Waters.* New York: Simon & Schuster, 1988.

Brockman, John, ed. *The New Humanists.* New York: Barnes & Noble, 2003.

Bstan-'dzin-rgya-mtsho, Dalai Lama XIV. *The Way to Freedom.* San Francisco: HarperSanFrancisco, 1994.

Buck-Morss, Susan. *The Origin of Negative Dialectics.* New York: Free Press, 1977.

Charters, Ann. *Kerouac: A Biography.* New York: St. Martin's Press, 1994.

Chesterton, G. K. *The Everlasting Man.* New York: Dodd, Mead, 1925.

_____. *Lunacy and Letters.* Ed. Dorothy Collins. New York: Sheed & Ward, 1958.

_____. *Outline of Sanity.* London: Methuen, 1928.

_____. *Tremendous Trifles.* London: Methuen, 1909.

_____. *What's Wrong with the World.* London: Cassell, 1910.

_____. *William Blake.* London: Duckworth, 1910.

Christy, Jim. *The Long, Slow Death of Jack Kerouac.* Toronto: ECW Press, 1998.

Clapp, Rodney. *Border Crossings.* Grand Rapids: Brazos Press, 2000.

Cohen, Leonard. *Stranger Music.* New York: Vintage, 1993.

Crowley, Donald, and Sue Mitchell Crowley, eds. *Critical Essays on Walker Percy.* Boston: G. K. Hall, 1989.

Davie, Donald, and Angela Livingstone. *Pasternak.* London: Macmillan, 1969.

Day, Dorothy. "More about Holy Poverty." *Catholic Worker* (February 1945): 1–2.

_____. "All the Way to Heaven Is Heaven." *Catholic Worker* (June 1948): 1, 2, 7.

_____. "Are the Leaders Insane?" *Catholic Worker* (April 1954): 1, 6.

Derrida, Jacques. *On Cosmopolitanism and Forgiveness*. New York: Routledge, 2001.

Dillenberger, Jane Daggett. *The Religious Art of Andy Warhol*. New York: Continuum, 1998.

Donaldson, Scott, ed. *Kerouac: On the Road—Text and Criticism*. New York: Penguin, 1979.

Dostoyevsky, Fyodor. *The Brothers Karamazov*. Trans. Constance Garnett. New York, London: W. W. Norton, 1976 [1880].

_____. *Notes from Underground*. Trans. Mirra Ginsburg. Intro. Donald Fanger. New York: Bantam Classic, 1989 [1864].

Eagleton, Terry. *Literary Theory*. Minneapolis: University of Minnesota Press, 1983.

Ellul, Jacques. *A Critique of Commonplaces*. Trans. Helen Weaver. New York: Knopf, 1966.

_____. *Living Faith*. New York: Harper & Row, 1980.

_____. *The New Demons*. New York: Seabury Press, 1975.

_____. *The Politics of God and the Politics of Man*. Grand Rapids: Eerdmans, 1972.

_____. *Propaganda*. New York: VintageBooks, 1973.

_____. *The Subversion of Christianity*. Trans. Geoffrey W. Bromiley. Grand Rapids: Eerdmans, 1986.

_____. *The Technological Society*. Trans. John Wilkinson. New York: Knopf, 1964.

_____. *What I Believe*. Trans. Geoffrey W. Bromiley. Grand Rapids: Eerdmans, 1989.

Fasching, Darrell J. *The Thought of Jacques Ellul: A Systematic Exposition*. New York: E. Mellen Press, 1981.

Frank, Joseph. *Dostoevsky. The Miraculous Years, 1865–1871*. Princeton, N.J.: Princeton University Press, 1995.

Frye, Northrop. *Anatomy of Criticism: Four Essays*. Princeton, N.J.: Princeton University Press, 1957.

_____. *Fearful Symmetry, A Study of William Blake*. Princeton, N.J.: Princeton University Press, 1948.

_____. *The Great Code: The Bible and Literature*. New York: Harcourt Brace, 1982.

_____. *The Modern Century: The Whidden Lectures 1967*. Toronto: Oxford University Press, 1967.

_____. *Northrop Frye on Religion*. Ed. Alvin A. Lee and Jean O'Grady. Toronto: University of Toronto Press, 2000.

_____. *Northrop Frye's Late Notebooks, 1982–1990: Architecture of the Spiritual World*. Ed. Robert D. Denham. Toronto: University of Toronto Press, 2000.

_____. *Spiritus Mundi: Essays on Literature, Myth, and Society*. Bloomington: Indiana University Press, 1976.

_____. *Stubborn Structure*. Ithaca, N.Y.: Cornell University Press, 1970.

Gans, Eric. *Signs of Paradox*. Stanford, Calif.: Stanford University Press, 1997.

Giamo, Ben. *Kerouac: The Word and the Way*. Carbondale: Southern Illinois University Press, 2000.

Gifford, Paul, et al., eds. *2000 Years and Beyond: Faith, Identity, and the Common Era*. London and New York: Routledge, 2003.

Girard, René. *Deceit, Desire, and the Novel: Self and Other in Literary Structure*. Trans. Yvonne Freccero. Baltimore: Johns Hopkins University Press, 1984.

_____. *Resurrection from the Underground*. Trans. James G. Williams. New York: Crossroad, 1997.

_____. *The Scapegoat*. Trans. Yvonne Freccero. Baltimore: Johns Hopkins University Press, 1986.

_____. *Things Hidden since the Foundation of the World*. Trans. Stephen Bann and Michael Metteer. Stanford, Calif.: Stanford University Press, 1987.

_____. *Violence and the Sacred*. Trans. Patrick Gregory. Baltimore: Johns Hopkins University Press, 1977.

Goethe, Johann Wolfgang von. *Maxims and Reflections*. New York: Penguin, 1999.

Gordon, W. Terrence. *Marshall McLuhan: Escape into Understanding*. New York: Basic Books, 1997.

Hardt, Michael, and Antonio Negri. *Empire*. Boston: Harvard University Press, 2001.

Hesse, Herman. *In Sight of Chaos*. Trans. Stephen Hudson. Zurich: Verlag Seldwyla, 1923.

Holmes, John Clellon. *Nothing More to Declare*. New York: Dutton, 1967 [1958].

Illich, Ivan. *ABC: The Alphabetization of the Popular Mind*. San Francisco: North Point Press, 1988.

_____. "An Address to 'Master Jacques.'" *Ellul Forum* 13 (July 1994): 16.

_____. *The Corruption of Christianity: Ivan Illich on Gospel, Church and Society.* Presented by David Cayley. Montreal: Canadian Broadcasting Corporation, 2000.

_____. *The Humiliation of the Word.* Trans. Joyce Main Hanks. Grand Rapids: Eerdmans, 1985.

_____. *In the Mirror of the Past: Lectures and Addresses, 1978–1990.* New York: M. Boyars, 1992.

_____. *Ivan Illich in Conversation.* Ed. David Cayley. Concord, Ont: Anansi, 1992.

_____. *Tools for Conviviality.* New York: Harper & Row, 1973.

James, William. "The Will to Believe." In *The Writings of William James,* ed. John J. McDermott, sec. 9. New York: Random House, 1967.

Joyce, James. *Portrait of the Artist as a Young Man.* New York: Penguin, 2003 [1910].

Kahn, Ashley. *A Love Supreme: The Story of John Coltrane's Signature Album.* New York: Viking, 2002.

Kaplan, Robert D. *Warrior Politics: Why Leadership Demands a Pagan Ethos.* New York: Random House, 2002.

Kenner, Hugh. *Paradox in Chesterton.* New York: Sheed & Ward, 1947.

Kerouac, Jack. *Kerouac: Selected Letters 1940–1956.* Ed. Anne Charters. New York: Penguin, 1996.

_____. *On the Road.* New York: Viking, 1957.

_____. *The Portable Jack Kerouac.* Ed. Anne Charters. New York: Penguin, 1996.

_____. *Satori in Paris.* New York: Grove Press, 1966.

_____. *Some of the Dharma.* New York: Penguin, 1997.

Kierkegaard, Søren. *Christian Discourses.* Trans. Walter Lowrie. Princeton, N.J.: Princeton University Press, 1971.

King, Martin Luther Jr. *Strength to Love.* Philadelphia: Fortress Press, 1986 [1963].

_____. *Testament of Hope.* Ed. James M. Washington. San Francisco: Harper & Row, 1986.

_____. *The Words of Martin Luther King, Jr.* Ed. Coretta Scott King. New York: Newmarket Press, 1987.

Kundera, Milan. *The Art of the Novel.* Trans. Linda Asher. New York: Perennial Library, 1988.

Kushner, Harold. *Who Needs God?* New York: Fireside Books, 2002.

Lardas, John. *The Bop Apocalypse.* Urbana: University of Illinois Press, 2001.

Lukacs, Georg. *The Theory of the Novel.* Trans. Anna Bostock. Cambridge: MIT Press, 1971.

Marx, Steven. *The Bible and Shakespeare.* New York: Oxford University Press, 2000.

McCann, Dennis P. *Christian Realism and Liberation Theology.* Maryknoll, N.Y.: Orbis Books, 1982.

McCarraher, Eugene. *Christian Critics: Religion and the Impasses in Modern American Social Thought.* Ithaca, N.Y.: Cornell University Press, 2000.

McLuhan, Marshall. *Counter Blast.* New York: Harcourt, Brace & World, 1969.

_____. *Culture Is Our Business.* New York: McGraw-Hill, 1970.

_____. *The Gutenberg Galaxy: The Making of Typographic Man.* Toronto: University of Toronto Press, 1962.

_____. *Letters of Marshall McLuhan.* Selected and ed. Matie Molinaro, Corrine McLuhan, and William Toye. Toronto: Oxford University Press, 1987.

_____. *The Medium and the Light: Reflections of Religion.* Ed. Eric McLuhan and Jacek Szlarek. Toronto: Stoddart, 1999.

_____ with Quentin Fiore. *The Medium Is the Message.* New York: Simon & Schuster, 1967.

_____. "Futurechurch: Edward Wakin Interviews Marshall McLuhan." *US Catholic* 42:1 (Jan. 1977): 6–11.

Merton, Thomas. *Conjectures of a Guilty By-Stander.* Garden City, N.Y.: Doubleday, 1966.

_____. *Contemplative Prayer.* Garden City, N.Y.: Doubleday, 1971.

_____. *Disputed Questions.* New York: Harcourt Brace Jovanovich, 1985.

_____. *Faith and Violence.* Notre Dame, Ind.: University of Notre Dame Press, 1968.

_____. *The Hidden Ground of Love.* Ed. William H. Shannon. New York: Harcourt Brace Jovanovich, 1985.

_____. *Ishi Means Man.* Greensboro, N.C.: Unicorn Press, 1976.

_____. *Literary Essays.* New York: New Directions, 1981.

_____. *Passion for Peace: The Social Essays.* Ed. William H. Shannon. New York: Crossroad, 1995.

_____. *The Seven Storey Mountain.* New York: Harcourt Brace Jovanovich, 1976 [1948].

_____. *Zen and the Birds of Appetite.* New York: New Directions, 1968.

Milosz, Cezslaw. *The Land of Ulro*. Trans. Louis Iribarne. New York: Farrar, Straus, & Giroux, 1984.

Murphy, Daniel. *Christianity and Modern European Literature*. Dublin and Portland, Oreg.: Four Courts Press, 1997.

Niebuhr, Reinhold. *The Nature and Destiny of Man: A Christian Interpretation*. Vol. 2. New York: Charles Scribner's Sons, 1964 [1943].

Pagels, Elaine. *The Gnostic Gospels*. New York: Vintage Books, 1989.

Paglia, Camille. *Vamps & Tramps*. New York: Vintage Books, 1994.

Pasternak, Boris. *Prose & Poems*. Ed. Stefan Schimanski. London: E. Benn, 1959.

Paz, Octavio. *Labyrinth of Solitude*. Trans. Lysander Kemp. New York: Grove Press, 1961.

Pearce, Joseph. *Literary Converts: Spiritual Inspiration in an Age of Unbelief*. San Francisco: Ignatius Press, 1999.

Percy, Walker. *Lost in the Cosmos: The Last Self-Help Book*. New York: Picador, 1983.

_____. *The Message in the Bottle*. New York: Farrar, Straus & Giroux, 1975.

_____. *The Moviegoer*. New York: Vintage Books, 1998 [1961].

_____. *Signposts in a Strange Land*. New York: Picador, 1991.

Polanyi, Karl. *The Great Transformation*. Boston: Beacon Press, 1964.

Poteat, Patricia Lewis. *Walker Percy and the Old Modern Age*. Baton Rouge: Lousiana State University Press, 1985.

Richards, I. A. *Coleridge on Imagination*. London: Routledge & Kegan Paul, 1950.

Roth, S.J., Robert J. *American Religious Philosophy*. New York: Harcourt, Brace & World, 1967.

Schumacher, E. F. *A Guide for the Perplexed*. London: J. Cape, 1977.

Solzhenitsyn, Aleksandr. *Gulag Archipelago: Volume One*. Trans. Thomas P. Whitney. New York: Harper, 1975.

_____. *The Oak and the Calf: Sketches of Literary Life in the Soviet Union*. Trans. Harry Willetts. New York: Harper & Row, 1975.

Stearn, Gerald Emanuel, ed. *McLuhan: Hot and Cool*. New York: New American Library, 1967.

Taylor, Ronald, ed. *Politics and Aesthetics*. London: Verso, 1977.

Theall, Donald. *The Virtual McLuhan*. Montreal and Kingston: McGill-Queens University Press, 2001.

Todd, Albert C., and Hayward, Max. *Twentieth Century Russian Poetry: Silver and Steel: An Anthology*. Selected by Yevgeny Yevtushenko. New York: Doubleday, 1994.

Tsvetaeva, Marina. *Art in the Light of Conscience*. Trans. Angela Livingstone. Cambridge: Harvard University Press, 1992.

Unamuno, Miguel de. *Tragic Sense of Life*. Trans. J. E. Crawford Flitch. New York: Dover Publications, 1954.

Vladislav, Jan, ed. *Václav Havel: Living in Truth*. London: Faber & Faber, 1989.

Webb, Eugene. *The Self Between: From Freud to the New Social Psychology of France*. Seattle: University of Washington Press, 1993.

Weil, Simone. *Gateway to God*. Glasgow: Collins, 1974.

_____. *The Simone Weil Reader*. Ed. George A. Panichas. New York: McKay, 1977.

Wolff, Edward N. *Top Heavy: A Study of the Increasing Inequality of Wealth in America*. New York: New Press, 2002.

Zizek, Slavoj. *The Fragile Absolute, or, Why Is the Christian Legacy Worth Fighting For?* London and New York: Verso, 2000.

Acknowledgments

A book like this one owes its existence to many books and to many conversations. I have been blessed with a great interlibrary loan department at Cal Poly, San Luis Obispo, and with many thoughtful friends who have helped me to think through the ideas presented here. And although it's impossible to name them all, I would like to thank those who helped me. Particular thanks goes to Bob Garlitz and Gary Cooper, who read very early drafts of this manuscript.

Thanks also to my colleagues and students in the English Department at California State Polytechnic University, San Luis Obispo, especially Allen Howell, Jim Cushing, Mark Roberts, Mike Wenzel, Dick Simon, George Cotkin, Paul Miklowitz, John Hampsey, David Kann, Linda Halisky, Tom Patchell, Suzanne Cokal, Tom Fay, Harry Hellenbrand, Joel Short, Ann Martin, Peter Gunther, Nick Sesnak, Randy Davis, Christopher Carruthers, Alison Halla, Deborah Lang, Steve Marx, Heidi Wilkinson, Glen Starkey, Andy Maness, Natalie Lambert, Mary Shannon, Alene Schultz, Nicole Biggers, Kelly Wooton, Melinda Moustakis, and Melanie Snowdy.

My cohorts at the Fetzer Foundation, especially Rob Lehman, Mark Nepo, Carolyn Brown, Parker J. Palmer, Cynthia Bourgealt, Jerry Needlham, Huston Smith, and Pam Wilson.

All of the fine scholars and writers that belong to the International Thomas Merton Society, especially Angus Stuart, Ross and Gisela Labrie, and Judith Hardcastle, for their hospitality, and to Roger Corliss, Christen Bochen, Bonnie Thurston, Paul Pearson, Patrick O'Connell, James Finley and Richard Rohr, for sharing their time and thoughts with me.

My fellow oblates of the New Comaldoli Monastery at Big Sur, especially Rita King, Hunter Lillis, Tory Haag, Larry Balthaser, and Paula and Mike Huston.

The Reverend Gary James and the Midwestern Unitarian Pastors' Association, for inviting me to one of their annual retreats.

My "other" family at the Cal Poly Newman Catholic Center: Sister Mary Pat White, Father Kevin and Father John, Father Mike and Sister Theresa, Ken Brown, and the students who went with me on our life-changing cross-cultural treks to Tijuana, especially Kevin Wilkinson, Ann Forester, Pasco and Meghan Bowen, Monica Inchausti, Andrea Dizinno, Cecilia Rodriguez, Tommy Jimenez, Christian Gnagne, Coung Nguyen, Preston and Jeanine Smalley, and Mike Ross.

Also Jim Hoffman and the people of Esperanza International, who made those trips possible, especially Sergio and Eduardo. Esperanza International is doing many of the things E. F. Schumacher and Wendell Berry recommend: focusing upon long-lasting solution to Third World poverty by providing a coordinated combination of development services that meet the needs of the poorest of the poor, including microenterprise development, education, vocational training, and health care. You can visit their Web site at www.esperanza.org.

And finally, thanks go to my editors, who have taught me so much, especially Rodney Clapp and Rebecca Cooper at Brazos Press.

Index